40 FOR 40

D1522479

40 FOR 40

Forty stories, sayings, and lessons learned from a non-celebrity, Costco-shopping, minivan-driving, extremely grateful married father of 5 kids who is turning forty years old

DENNIS O'DONNELL

40 for 40
Copyright © 2022 by Dennis O'Donnell
dfodonnell3@gmail.com

All rights reserved
No portion of this book may be reproduced, stored in a retrieval system, or transmitted
in any form by any means–electronic, mechanical, photocopy, recording, or other–except
for brief quotations in printed reviews, without prior permission of the author.

First Edition

Hardcover ISBN: 979-8-84582-025-9
Paperback ISBN: 979-8-84789-515-6

Dedicated to Colleen, Declan, Evelyn, Maggie, Frannie, and Daniel.

Nothing means more to me than being part of your family.

CHAPTERS

FORTY FOR FORTY

"Who in the *absolute hell* would read a book written by you? You're not a reality TV star. You're not a famous CEO. You're not a Bitcoin speculator, a professional athlete, or an Instagram fitness model. In fact, you don't even have Instagram. Or Facebook. Or TikTok or Tumblr or WeChat. You shoot a 126 when you play golf by the rules, you've driven the same minivan for 9 years, you're at Costco enough to receive your mail there, and the best job you've ever had involved selling toilet paper. Explain to me again who would want to hear your story?"

Welp…at this moment, those are all true statements. And even though no one has said each of those sentences consecutively (that I am aware of), that's likely because I never told anyone that I was writing a book. Had I mentioned that I was writing a book like this one, that's pretty much the response I would have expected to receive.

Sometimes it's better just to do the work.

After celebrating my 38th birthday with family and friends, I began dedicating time to writing down a few of the meaningful experiences I've had and the path that I'd come from, recalling some of the mistakes I've made, thinking about the fun experiences I've had, and reflecting on the lessons and progress that have taken place over my first 40 years. The approach of decade birthdays seems to cause people to think a little more introspectively about the path they're on and how they're living, and this was no different for me.

From there, I began crafting a better understanding of the vision and goals I wanted for myself over the next 40 years that I could strive for. Those exercises slowly came together and turned into an effort I thought would be better suited as a long-form story that I could talk about with my wife, Colleen, and our 5 young kids together to spark conversations and allow us to get to know each other in a more intimate way.

This is the type of activity that I've always heard was extremely helpful for people to do when setting a vision for themselves, but one that I never got around to doing before…sort of like flossing twice a day, or not eating bacon.

Along the way, I discovered there was something very appealing to me about writing out stories of a life that many outsiders might consider "average" on first glance. I have never considered my own life "average" in any way and believe it to be quite big with a great deal of impact and meaning to myself and those around me. But my guess is that without qualitative societal indicators like fame, celebrity, riches, status, and adoration from the masses, mine and others like it are lives that could mistakenly be dismissed as ordinary by outsiders—and I just don't agree with the supposition, at all.

I noticed that I began feeling protective of the incredible people I have met. I wanted to write out a few stories from my life and share them in hopes that others connect to them and see their own lives as more than just "normal" or "average," even though they may not be movie stars or have millions of followers on social media. There is so much more that makes a life meaningful than what our global society seems to have gravitated toward, and I think it's important to slow down and remember that the most fulfilling parts of your existence rarely show up in a Google search result.

Most people I've come across have a few heroic stories in them, which would grip and inspire the masses, involving the daily individual battles they've silently fought and won if they were able to clearly articulate them and if others were curious enough to learn about them. There are significant achievements and personal obstacles that your spouse and children and best friend and neighbor and co-worker are dealing with that you are completely unaware of—and some are facing them with the kind of courage and fortitude that you read about in Greek Mythology to get themselves through it all. I know that because I've been through them myself and I find the journey worthy of discussion.

I am hopeful that the stories and ideas in this book are an indicator of personal progress demonstrating that I am formulating the type of thoughts, aim, and most importantly actions to move closer toward the best version of myself as days and years continue to go by. This comes from a father and husband first and foremost trying to create a big and loving and supportive world for myself and my family. This comes from an individual who has endured quite a few twists and turns and potholes along this journey, striving like hell and struggling on the quest to move toward "the good." And this comes from someone who is trying to make the many communities I am part of better and stronger than they would be without me.

I am hopeful that this book contains more knowledge to convey than it would if I had written it when I was turning 20 years old. And I really hope that this book will be a far worse version than the book that I could write when I eventually turn 60 years old. Or even when I turn 41 years old, for that matter. The primary goal I have developed is to keep moving in the right direction and forever reset myself to a better version as days go on, even as major setbacks occur.

One of the things I talk with my kids about frequently is the importance of living a "Big Life." My idea on living a "Big Life" is one based on love, passion, purpose, and responsibility. Giving and receiving authentic, honest love makes you Big. Taking on meaningful responsibility and being accountable to it makes you Big. Pursuing what brings fulfillment to yourself and improves the life of others around you, becoming the strongest and best possible version of yourself makes you Big and compounds your size exponentially.

My life has been getting Bigger as our family continues to grow, and I want to continue making it as beautiful and meaningful as I can, as long as I am still living. To date, it's been one that contains a well-balanced assortment of challenges, disappointments, failures, successes, resilience, adventure, service, growth, and love, I am hopeful that by sharing a few of the stories I've lived, you will be able to see part of them in your own story, as well.

I do not remember much about what kind of life I envisioned for myself growing up. I didn't ever give it much thought, to be honest. But I really love the one I am living right now, and I could not be more grateful for the blessings I have received—none more so than marrying Colleen and having the chance to share every experience with her and our having the honor to bring five of the most amazing kids into the world. I want to do my best to take advantage of these and other blessings, to recognize them as they appear, to appreciate them, to cultivate them, and to make the most out of every opportunity that comes our way.

Thank you for reading this book. I hope you enjoy.

CHAPTER 2

LESSONS FROM LOU

Salmon need very little encouragement to swim upstream. The sun needs very little encouragement to rise in the east each day. And from experience, I can also say that kids growing up near South Bend, Indiana, need very little encouragement to become faithful fans of Notre Dame football.

When I was a kid, I *idolized* this team. I loved everything about the school and the program, and I assigned the absolute highest moral and physical attributes to each player, coach, and manager who was on the sidelines on game day. The blue jerseys, the gold helmets, listening to Jack Nolan calling games on the radio, the aura and mystique around campus. Everything. I simply could not get enough.

When my friends and I would play pickup basketball and pretend to be NBA players, I would ask that they call me "Rocket Ismail" (star wide receiver and kick returner) instead of Michael Jordan. I had pictures of Tony Rice, Chris Zorich, Jerome Bettis, Rick Mirer, Kevin McDougall, and hundreds of others posted everywhere throughout my room and frequently tried to tack them around the kitchen, hoping my mom wouldn't notice. But since we lived near South Bend, even if she did notice, the pictures were rarely taken down and were instead seen as a nice upgrade to complement the *Feng Shui* of the area.

This team won a National Championship in 1988 when I was 6 years old—which is a prime time to cement one's lifelong loyalty and passion if you're a fan. It also didn't hurt that I was raised by a dad who threw the single greatest tailgate party at every home game for 30 years and made watching the game on TV in a grass parking lot outside the baseball field an event far more memorable and enjoyable than going inside the actual stadium.

It shouldn't be a surprise, then, to learn that one of my favorite memories from my childhood stems directly from Notre Dame football. The 1993 season had been magical. I was 11 years old as the year was winding down, and ND appeared destined to win its second national championship in five years if they could slay the undefeated Florida State Seminoles, who were coming into South Bend on November 13, 1993, in an epic #1 vs. #2 showdown that had the entire nation's undivided attention.

Most fans are familiar with the result of the game—it remains one of most indelible experiences for the Notre Dame faithful that were there or watched the game from afar—but what was most memorable for me happened a day before kickoff, on November 12, 1993.

My dad, being the super-fan that he was, would host tons of people at his tailgate parties each weekend, and often the attendees would reciprocate his hospitality by offering him game tickets or experiences around campus to show their gratitude. One previous party attendee happened to have access to the Notre Dame Monogram Club Luncheon, where a large consortium of players, coaches, fans, and program supporters gather on campus at the Joyce Center for lunch the day before a home game to build spirit and momentum heading into the weekend. But this game against FSU was not just any game—when FSU came into town in 1993, it was *the game*, and getting to attend *this* luncheon was truly special.

So, my dad accepted the offer and did what any good father and responsible caretaker would do—he pulled me out of school that day so I could participate in one the coolest events a kid could experience. The atmosphere walking into that luncheon was like nothing I'd experienced before, with so much excitement and hope and nervousness and joy from so many different people looking forward to one of the biggest college football games ever played.

We eventually found our table among a sea of hundreds. I sat down and pretended that I knew which of the four forks was proper to use at each point in the meal and tried not spill my drink when Head Coach Lou Holtz stepped up the microphone to address the crowd.

Lou Holtz.

The actual guy.

For context on how excited I was to be in the same room as Lou Holtz, two years before this event I was in 3rd grade, and on the first day of school I saw a large sign posted on the wall that read as follows:

"Treat People the Way You Want to Be Treated." —*Lou Holtz*

"Holy smokes," I thought to myself. "If Lou Holtz is wise enough to come up with such a beautiful and powerful statement like that—a thought that could literally lead to the entire world becoming a better place for people to live and love and flourish together—imagine how good a football coach he must be! He chose to *coach football* instead of becoming czar of the universe and leading billions of people to peace and prosperity, which means he's a really tremendous football coach!"

It took me far longer than I care to admit before I learned that Lou Holtz was not, in fact, the originator of that phrase and that it is the foundation of multiple philosophies and religions that go back thousands and thousands of years. Somebody named Jesus Christ, for example, was a prominent proponent of such a thought and was around quite a few years before Lou Holtz.

Looking back, it's clear to me that the poster I saw had to have been shipped exclusively to elementary schools within the greater Northern Indiana region and was printed by a proud Notre Dame alum…but then again, those are things I didn't quite realize on my first day of third grade.

The luncheon proceeds, and Lou Holtz takes the microphone. I am on the edge of my seat. I am waiting for the fire, and I am waiting for the brimstone. I am ready to be motivated, and I am ready to beat Florida State.

And then he starts speaking. But it's...weird. There is no yelling, there is no machismo, and there are none of the pyrotechnics happening in the background that I 100 percent expected to see.

"Let me tell you the three questions I ask each player before he comes to play football for me at the University of Notre Dame," he began. Not quite the rah-rah inspirational talk I thought was coming, but I decided to give him a shot and listen.

"Can I trust you? Do you care about me? And are you committed to excellence? That's it. Just those three. Obviously, you've got to be able to play the game of football pretty well to come to a university like this, too, but if you're the best player in the nation and we can't find alignment on these three questions, you will have to find somewhere else to play college football as long as I am the head coach at Notre Dame."

I will stop using quotation marks, so I don't give the impression I remember every single word verbatim from his speech, but in general here is how he broke each question down and explained why they were important to his team's success:

Can I Trust You?

Lou was saying this as a football coach in the context of building a successful team, but he was quick to point out that trust is the most critical component of every meaningful relationship you will have with people in every facet of your life. You can't have a successful marriage, or lasting friendships, or professional relationships, or relationships with your children, etc., without both sides fully trusting each other. For a relationship to grow and strengthen, there must be alignment on what trust means, and effort must be demonstrated so trust can be cultivated to ensure you're working toward someone else's best interests. Trust also allows people to have more honest and sometimes more difficult conversations to get each other back on the right track, knowing that the person you're talking to genuinely has your best interests at heart… those kinds of constructive conversations can be only as effective as the level of trust that exists between those speaking to each other.

Do You Care About Me?

Teams and relationships will work best when members feel that they are more than a means to an end, more than a cog in the wheel, and more than a disposable resource that can be easily replaced. This requires people to demonstrate a level of empathy and consideration for others as individuals, as someone who matters, and as someone who is valued for what their unique capabilities and skillsets can bring to the group. This doesn't mean we have to be best friends, or even friends—but it does mean that you have to care about me, my needs as an individual, and the life I lead away from our partnership. You need to recognize that there is more to me than what you're aware of. When you notice someone on your team struggling in their performance and you care enough to dig in, you often realize the source of frustration and pain stems from outside the team environment or the job. Life is big and complex and things can go wrong in a variety of ways for people physically and emotionally. Demonstrating care only helps build the kind of relationship necessary to develop a successful partnership.

Are You Committed to Excellence?

We're here working together. We've got the same goals, and our incentives are aligned. We trust each other, and we care about each other. Now, the question becomes, are we willing to provide the effort necessary to stretch ourselves and become the best possible version of ourselves to achieve our shared goals? Are we going to mail this in and do just enough to complete a task, or are we going to maximize our collective behaviors to bring out the best in each other? I love this question because it is something that only you can answer honestly— what is your personal best (knowing that your personal best will vary depending on your health or situation in any moment) and are you reaching it? No one else on earth can know the true answer except you—but asking the question should signal the intent to pursue something meaningfully and with dedication to a favorable outcome.

After Lou finished explaining his thoughts around the Three Questions, he began wrapping up the speech. Not much had been said about the opponent that week. Did he forget that his team was playing Florida State?

"I should probably go up on stage and remind him about Charlie Ward, FSU's Heisman candidate quarterback that we have to stop," I thought to myself.

Lou stated, "In closing, I want to remind this group of one more thing: the best gift you can possibly give your children is showing them how much you love your spouse."

All right, that's it. Now was obviously the time for me to step in and get this ship back on track. "Lou, seriously—this is a really big game. We need to win this one to get another national championship. FSU is like, really good at playing football; we need a strategy, not a Hallmark card," I said to myself.

I don't recall many of the plays of the game the following day—a few pop into mind when I see replays come on TV or if I hear people describing them in detail. I remember tailgating with my parents and enjoying one of my favorite days as a young fan on campus that weekend.

But those three questions, and the comment about showing your children how much you love your spouse? I think about those almost *every single day*. Those questions have impacted the way I act, and they've made me a better husband, a better professional, a better friend, and a better man when I keep them at the front of my mind.

I talk about these three questions often with the teams I lead in my job, and when I discuss them I am also expecting that my team is asking the same questions of me. This makes me structure my words and behaviors to ensure that I am someone who can be trusted, someone who genuinely cares, and someone who is committed to giving their best at all times. When I trust my team members, I don't have to micromanage them, and when they trust me, they know I will be there to help guide them and coach them whenever necessary. When they know I care about them, it helps us communicate more authentically, more frequently, and more meaningfully—which undeniably brings better results. And when we work our tails off to try to ensure that the result is the best one possible, we can rest easy and let the chips fall where they may, because we know that we gave our personal best.

Who knows…maybe the print shop that supplied my 3rd grade classroom with that faux-poster was onto something when they gave him credit for the quotation. That Lou guy turned out to be a pretty wise man, after all.

CHAPTER 3

"FUN TIME IS OVER, MAN."

Toward the end of summer following fifth grade, I found myself ter-
rified at the prospect of going to middle school. I had a few older
friends in the neighborhood whom I hung out with, and all I heard
from them during the months of July and August was a version of the
following:

"Dude, you just wait. You had it so easy in elementary school.
When you get to middle school, all that changes. It's going to be much,
much harder and most of your classmates won't make it through. Trust
me. Fun time is over, man."

And with that, those wise sages would place a couple sweet pogs
inside their Guess Jeans pockets and ride off into the sunset on their
Schwinn 10-speeds that had a Chicago Bears QB Mike Tomczak Fleer
Card placed in the spokes to make sure everyone could not only see
but also hear just how cool they were. They were confident they had
imparted all the foresight and acumen they could onto the younger
generation; their jobs were now complete.

The worst part about this, aside from the fact that pogs were ever
popular with people I spent time with, is that I believed them. Some of

the teachers I had in fifth grade had echoed a similar sentiment through-out the previous school year and it seemed like a credible threat. So I entered the hallowed halls of Grissom Middle School as a sixth grader that fall far more nervous than I should have been about what lay ahead.

"Am I smart enough to make it all the way through sixth grade? If it's as bad as they say it is, will I even have time to play sports? Or will there be too much homework and calculus to complete? I wonder if I will ever see my family and those same cool older friends again? I sure hope so because they've been *so helpful* in letting me know how difficult everything was going to be. Thank goodness they were there to give me the warning."

The first few weeks of sixth grade went by, and I went on to meet the best new friends I could imagine. I had happy and thoughtful teachers that loved their job, and lo and behold wouldn't you know it, I still had plenty of time to see my buddies and play all the sports I wanted to.

Hmm...

"Surely, it must be the *second half* of the school year they were talking about," I thought to myself. "I bet that's when it *really* gets hard. Then the fun time will be over, man. For sure."

And while I was waiting for the other shoe to drop, the second half of sixth grade came and went. And again, the experience I was having was pretty amazing. Then the same thing happened in seventh grade, and eventually eighth grade. All of it was downright fantastic. Were there some not-so-fun challenges I came across during that time? Yep. Was every part of it different from what I experienced in elementary school? Yep. But it was great, and I felt like a fool for listening to a bunch of knuckleheads a few summers back and letting them convince me that I was in for a terrible experience.

When I was preparing for ninth grade, the same type of messages continued coming at me from all sorts of different people. "Oh man, high school—this is where it *really* gets difficult. All that stuff you got away with in middle school doesn't fly anymore. This is going to be so much harder. Trust me. Fun time is over, man."

Rinse. Repeat. Same thing. All I experienced was a fun, new, awkward, challenging, and wonderful time getting through all of it just like everyone else was. Were there some seriously low lows? Yep. Was it different than middle school? Yep. But it was better, too, and I loved the experience despite all the pitfalls I encountered along the way.

As I got older and began approaching new milestones, it never failed that I would hear from someone swooping in out of right field to tell me how difficult it was going to be, or that I shouldn't do it, or that fun time was over.

Getting that first job out of college? "Welcome to the *real world,* buddy. You just wait and see. Trust me. Fun time is over, man."

Getting married? "Pssh. That's it. Game over. No more friends for you. Trust me. Fun time is over, man."

Having your first child? "Say goodbye to sleeping and your social life. Trust me. Fun time is over, man."

Taking that big promotion at work? "You're taking over the worst division in the company, no one succeeds there. Trust me. Fun time is over, man."

Having your second, third, fourth, and fifth child? "Uhh…wait, seriously? You have five kids? You probably haven't had any real fun in like a decade. So, I guess it's *been over*, man."

You get the gist.

I have learned that there are always going to be people waiting in the wings to tell you how difficult something is going to be or explain why you shouldn't do whatever cool thing it is you're embarking on. Some of these people have good intentions and are trying to help you avoid failure based on their previous experiences, while others project fear and uncertainty only to hold you in your place so they don't feel worse when you succeed.

Is adjusting to your first job, or getting married, or having children or taking on a huge new role at work challenging? Hell yes, there are plenty of times when all those things can be difficult. Any time you take on more responsibility and accountability in life there are going to be challenges associated with it that were not present prior to your doing so. But I am happy to attest that despite the challenges associated with these responsibilities, there's still plenty of joy and fulfillment and fun to be had along the way—I would suggest even more so, because that responsibility you're carrying leads to deeper meaning for you in the process of working your way through it all.

When we accept unjustified fears or negativity from others as truth, it limits us from developing what is possible on our own path. There are no two circumstances people can compare in precise fashion. It takes courage to disregard that fear being thrown on you and take strong steps forward with the confidence that your path will be your own.

I remember having a conversation with an aunt I was very close with as I was talking through some of the nerves I was dealing with when preparing for college. She explained that she had a great time when she was in college, but that she enjoyed her life after school even more, and she expected that trend to continue because she was empowered with the proper way to frame the next steps she was taking along the way. She listened thoughtfully and took her time as she clearly and lovingly stated to me, "Life keeps getting better as you get older. Don't let anyone ever tell you otherwise."

I wanted that to be true when I heard her say it because I loved the idea that there was always something meaningful and fulfilling to look forward to, and because it was such a different idea than what I had heard from anyone up to that point in my life. I thought it was beautiful and it became something I wanted to make a reality for the life I was leading.

There are new and different challenges you will encounter with each new milestone or step you take...some of these steps will take you higher, some will take you backward or sideways, and some steps are more difficult than others. But I think we'd be wise to ignore the fear others unnecessarily try putting on us to justify the limits they've put on their own adventure and embrace the idea that life can keep getting better as you move on to whatever new paths you choose to pursue on your journey.

CHAPTER 4

EXPERIENCES ARE
BETTER THAN THINGS

I can already see the angrily crossed arms and contemptuous stares coming at me from the 4- to 16-year-old demographic when they hear this, but as I've gotten older, I've learned that Experiences Are Better Than Things, and I really don't think it's a close competition between the two.

People of all ages put in a herculean amount of time and effort and stress to make birthdays and holidays and anniversaries as special as they can for their loved ones. One of the largest stressors we have around these occasions usually involves shopping for gifts. We put pressure on ourselves by believing that the level of care and affection we have for someone is directly associated with the type of present we provide to them. If we want to prove that we love someone very much, we must get them lots of expensive gifts, and if we don't, then it must mean we don't care about them very much—something like that.

Christmas season is the Super Bowl, Olympics, and World Cup all rolled into one when it comes to this kind of thinking. Throughout the first few weeks of December, each child's anticipation for Christmas Day is unsurpassed by any other feeling. Each activity they participate in seems geared toward the morning they get to open all the new things awaiting them under the tree. Those weeks can be minefields for adults and parents who are driving themselves into the ground to make sure that each wish is perfectly fulfilled and that each person on their list gets each of the exact presents that was requested to create the best possible day for them.

And on that morning, when the kids wake up at 5 a.m. after not sleeping a wink, having tried their best to get a sneak peek at Santa Claus roaming their hallways, there is real magic in the air while gift wrap and bows are flying in each direction, and everyone is discovering the fun new gifts added to their arsenal from Santa and others. It is a beautiful and wondrous moment, months in the making, that we believe we will collectively cherish forever.

But in a span of just a few hours, the magic that was created around the opening of most gifts seems to fade. That doesn't mean that people who receive the gifts are ungrateful or aren't provided some level of happiness with the presents they receive. But the excitement of what was to come often exceeds the moment itself, and if we're being honest, there can even be a bit of an emotional letdown when you're staring at the pile of gifts once everything is said and done.

I would guess that my kids don't remember most of the individual presents they received for Christmas over the past 3 or 4 years. There were a lot of kids and a lot of gifts, so perhaps the reason they can't remember them has to do with the quantity of what was received, but I have a sneaking suspicion that it's more likely that once the gift was opened and played with for a while, the meaningfulness of the present was no longer as strong as the anticipation that led to receiving it. They were grateful for the presents, and I think they enjoyed them for a bit, but I don't think most were very memorable.

I do know that my kids can tell you every detail about the trip we took to Dollywood during that time. I know they can paint you a picture highlighting every ride they went on and every character they got a picture with when we went to Disney World together as a family during that time. I know they can describe every bite of the ice cream and what color slushies they had after a day spent on the beaches of Indiana Dunes during that time.

They can tell you nearly everything that happened when we attended a Kane County Cougars baseball game during that time. They can tell you details about the beautiful dresses they saw at one of the musicals attended at a local high school during that time. And they can tell you everything you would ever want to know about the Van Gogh Immersive Art Exhibit they walked through in the city for Frannie's sixth birthday.

They remember experiences far more than they remember gifts. I think we all do. Even the mediocre experiences get remembered and seem to have more meaning than some of the best gifts they've received.

There is just something so indelible about having shared experiences with people we love, and I've learned it's better when I prioritize these over physical gifts if I'm looking for ways to connect with others and show people that I care about them.

Things break. Things get lost. Things are easily forgotten. Things go out of style. Things are temporary.

Experiences stay with us forever. Experiences help us create stronger relationships with each other. Experiences put us in the deep end when it comes to meaning and help us define our passions.

When people pass away, we rarely think about the gifts we received from them. We remember the cherished times we spent with them and the experiences we shared—even the difficult or seemingly banal ones. We might hold more closely to a physical gift we received from them after they pass away, but that's primarily because we're not able to share any more experiences alongside them and it serves as a substitute in their memory.

In 2012, my team at work spent an entire year with our heads down developing one of the most important brand creations and product launches our client had ever put forth in their 100+ year history.

We were working morning, day, and night to ensure everything went off without a hitch, and we spent more time together than on any other project I have worked on since in my career.

Whenever I cross paths with anyone from that project today, the first thing they mention has nothing to do with the work we completed. The first thing they talk about with me is the time we decided to sneak away from a fancy dinner we were attending to watch Axl Rose and Guns n Roses play a live show in Las Vegas. It was a last second decision and it was totally unplanned, but we made it happen and, in the process, created one of the coolest memories of a work trip possible. Today, very few of us can recall the revenue projection details or workflows of that huge project with any specificity—but we remember almost every song from the set list that night and count ourselves lucky we were able to experience it together.

iPads and purses and cool new toys are great. Material goods can provide momentary pleasure and convenience, and we need a good majority of them to carry out our lives. But I've learned I can't expect to find true happiness through owning stuff alone compared with the fulfillment I derive from experiences.

Buy experiences with people—going to movies and sitting down for dinners and playing board games and taking walks to the park. Buy more time with hobbies you enjoy and leisurely activity with people you care about. Buy a family vacation. Buy a coffee and have a conversation with someone you want to connect with.

Experiences Are Better Than Things.

CHAPTER 5

GO FIND AN ADVENTURE

Alittle over 15 years ago I started hanging out with a group of guys whom I would quickly learn were some of the most seasoned outdoor adventurers I'd ever met. One of the first times I was with them, they were celebrating the return of a year-long sabbatical that stretched across Australia, New Zealand, Malaysia, Thailand, Cambodia, Vietnam, China, and Japan, which included the most unique and challenging explorations that anyone had ever described to me. I was about as inexperienced as one could be compared with them in these traveling activities, but I could feel myself becoming more and more interested in what they talked about when we were together and could tell that it was something I would likely enjoy if ever given the opportunity.

In 2007 they were planning their next excursion and I was hanging around them just frequently enough that they felt a guilty obligation to throw an offer my way. When they got around to asking me to accompany them to the summit of one of the highest mountains in the United States, I was excited and naïve enough to say yes without considering I hadn't done anything even remotely close to this before and had no idea how I would fare. They had their sights set on Mount

Langley, a 14,042-foot mountain located on the border of Sequoia National Park and the John Muir Wilderness in the heart of the Sierra Nevada Mountains in Southern California. A mountain is considered a "fourteener" if it has an elevation over 14,000 feet, which tends to make them more attractive for prospective adventurers to take on, and we were excited that we'd have a "fourteener" mark on our belts if we could accomplish our goal of getting to the top of Mount Langley. This mountain is located less than 5 miles away from the more well-known Mount Whitney, the highest mountain in the contiguous United States and the crown jewel of the Inyo National Forest.

This was the first backcountry hike I had ever taken, and everything about the preparation process associated with the trip felt exhilarating to me. Going to the REI in the city to buy gear was a new and eye-opening experience and made me realize how much ridiculously cool stuff is out there for those who are into the hobby. Setting my Out of Office up on my computer knowing that when people emailed me at work, I would be in an area with *zero reception* available—even if I wanted to connect—was a satisfying task to complete. And packing my bag knowing that whatever I chose to bring would be all that I had available to me for four days made me focus just a little more closely than when I would pack for my regular flights to Dallas or Memphis for work.

Sitting at their apartment a few days before we left and watching them pour themselves into a topography map, arguing about which trails would be best to use, somehow turned into a time machine to other trips they'd taken in the past and made me realize how much detailed planning goes into these hikes to maximize the chances of success. Each of them was so knowledgeable and had so much experience, which made it even funnier to hear them question each other's thought process and decision making while coming up with what would be the final plans for the group.

"Listen man, if we go through that route, we're gonna have another Tetons or Maroon Bells situation on our hands and everyone remembers how that went…we need to go a different direction, here take a look at what I'm thinking." I, of course, was clueless to whatever on God's green's earth any of that meant, but I nodded along in solidarity that the actions that took place in the Tetons and Maroon Bells that one time when I was 1,000 miles away should probably be avoided this time around.

On the day we finally arrived at the trailhead outside the town of Lone Pine, California, I had butterflies churning in my gut that I hadn't felt in years. My pack was filled to the brim with snacks, clothes, water bottles, and topped with a tent that I didn't practice setting up beforehand, so I was really hoping it would be in proper condition when the time eventually came for sleeping. I followed my friends' lead as we set forth on the first steps of what would be a three-day outdoor adventure along scenery and terrain that I'd never experienced but knew would be spectacular.

I was immediately surprised at how much I loved the solitude this type of activity provided. Even though I was right next to two other friends the entire time, I couldn't help but feel alone with my thoughts in the best possible way and was able to get a little more clarity around the larger opportunities and stressors I was facing in my life back home. My eyes remained focused on scaling the elevation gains while carrying an extra 50 pounds on my back and trying not to fall headfirst into a gaping ravine, but my head and heart were elsewhere on a higher plain and thoroughly enjoying the majesty around me and the emotions swirling within me.

After the first day of hiking, we setup camp and I learned what a "Jet Boil Dinner" was all about. It was my job to use the manual filtering device and make our water supply clean enough to cook with and drink from for the remainder of the evening. Filtering water from a stream is not a particularly difficult task to perform, but it is time consuming. You pump, and you pump, and you pump from the source. The water is then transferred from the tube that is dipping in the source through the filter inside the device. Of all the water that gets into the device, only a very small portion of it makes it through to your attached Nalgene bottle. You notice pretty quickly that most of the water you're pumping is filled with bacteria and other unhealthy elements that end up getting filtered away from the bottles you're attempting to fill.

I sat there for an hour filtering the water that evening and was mesmerized by the process, having no idea that my friends considered this something of a rookie hazing ritual and that it was a task they absolutely hated performing. They were annoyed at how happy and proud I was when I came back with six clean Nalgene bottles full of filtered water ready to be consumed without a clue that I had just been sent to do some good ol' fashioned grunt work.

The clean water was then placed into a Jet Boil, which is a cylindrical sleeved stove that utilizes a small portable isobutane gas can, a burner and igniter to bring water to the point of boiling within minutes. It is a genius invention and something every serious backpacker has in their repertoire of gear. When the water is ready, you pour the boiling water into a freeze-dried meal kit then quickly re-seal the pouch and set aside for 5-10 minutes allowing it to cook. After the cooking is complete, you drain the water and you're able to eat meals like Sesame Chicken, or Pesto Pasta, or Teriyaki Rice, or whatever glorious packet you were able to find at REI right from the bag with a fork and eat like royalty on top of a mountain without being anywhere close to a kitchen or restaurant. I wasn't sure if it was because this was my first time eating a Jet Boil Dinner and the novelty of it all was so fun, or because I was starving, but in that moment, it tasted better than anything I'd eaten in months.

I woke up at 3 a.m. to sit outside my tent alone and found myself looking up at the biggest and brightest night sky I had ever seen with more stars than I dreamed were possible shining brilliantly above. I considered for the first time how strange it was that this exact sky and these exact stars are always present but only fully visibly to those that live away from places like Chicago and all the light pollution they emit, which provides vast amounts of illumination on the ground and all but eliminates it above. It was sad for a moment to consider that I was 24 years old and had just seen this kind of sky for the first time, and somehow simultaneously comforting knowing it had been there the whole time for others to enjoy.

When we summited Mount Langley later in the trip, I looked down from the highest point I had ever been in my life and was awestruck at the view and how accomplished I felt. This was the sort of adventure that I didn't quite realize I had always wanted to do, and it became clear to me at that moment. I was very appreciative of my friends bringing me along to experience the journey.

By the time my flight from Los Angeles landed back in Chicago with my backpack far dirtier and lighter than it was when the trip started, and I lay my head on my pillow to sleep in my bed for the first time in five days, I was hooked. From there the backpacking trips became something we planned and would later think about together for years to come. I had officially made it "in" the hiking group, and I was beyond grateful for the chance to be part of it.

In 2008 we were scheduled to hike up Mount Hood near Portland, Oregon, but when we arrived on site the mountain was washed out with rain and covered with snow and all permits were made unavailable. We stopped at the house of my aunt, who lived nearby and looked through a map together to find another option since we were already there with all our gear and discovered the Wallowa Mountains, located in the Columbia Plateau of northeastern Oregon and a five-hour drive from where we were in Portland. We had some incredibly long days on this hike, one of which was due to blowing right past the first campsite without realizing it while pushing through and deciding we were too far ahead to turn around by the time we found out, so we essentially completed two days' worth of walking into one and were completely smoked when the time finally came to set up camp.

We got to take in the town of Hood River when our hike was over and stayed there for an evening before getting to the airport to return home, which just continued to illustrate how perfect the entire state of Oregon is when it comes to all things outdoors. This trip was also the first time I had ever come face-to-face with a full-grown elk, a moment I found to be terrifying while relieving myself near the bushes in complete darkness just past midnight on the second night of our trek.

In 2009 we tackled Yosemite National Park located in the central Sierra Nevada mountains of California. The first couple days were spent trying to wrap our minds around just how large and breathtaking ancient sequoia trees are, hiking out to the top of Eagle Point, walking carefully along the brutal edges and terrifying granite cliffs of the globally renowned El Capitan, and taking in the beauty within the North Rim Trail. We discovered the single most beautiful campsite any one of us had seen that stared across at Half Dome which provided one of the most stunning backdrops imaginable that we enjoyed while resting and relaxing together for one of the evenings. This is also the trip during which I decided to rock a pair of knock-off Jordan VI basketball shoes throughout the hike instead of the more common Columbia or Merrell brand options, which I was told was a rather unique decision and remains something I am made fun of to this day.

There are more than 800 miles of hiking trails in Yosemite and there is no way to do and see everything this wonderful place has to offer in one trip. I got a small taste of what makes this park so special this time around and saw why it draws 4 million visitors annually from all over the world. I cannot wait to return.

In 2010 we hiked through the North Cascades National Park in Washington state, near the Canadian border. During this excursion I recall our being at such a high elevation that at one point, when we stopped to take a break, I noticed we were sitting above a string of clouds. That kind of perspective isn't unusual when you're seated on an airplane looking downward, but to do so while on your own two feet was beyond cool. We had a great stroke of luck when securing our permits for that week because it turned out to be the only nights of the year that the Perseid Meteor Shower was clearly visible directly over our heads when we set up camp each night. As someone who had never seen a real-life meteor shower, this was another unbelievably unique experience that I was grateful to be part of. We walked through streams that were surrounded with dozens of large, wild pink salmon surrounding our every step as they continued their long trek upstream. After reading that last sentence it should come as little surprise to hear that we also had a horrifying encounter with a mama bear and her baby cub that was only about 50 yards ahead of us near this area which stopped us cold in our tracks for about 45 minutes until we felt that they had moved far enough away from where we were hiding.

Hiking enthusiasts love to talk about what to do when you encounter a bear…they often say things like "Make lots of noises, so the bear doesn't think you're sneaking up on it. Walk slowly. Make yourself big so the bear gets intimidated and doesn't want to engage you in a battle." Blah blah blah. All that ivory-tower wisdom goes completely out the window when you encounter a mother bear who is next to her baby cub. If that happens, my suggestion is that you curl into a tiny little ball inside of a humongous bush and pray to God that the mama is busy with a list of errands to take care of that afternoon that does not include "ripping a human being's face off with my paws" because if it does you're dead and there's nothing you can do about it.

In 2014 we got back together at Zion National Park in southwest Utah after a few years' hiatus that included each person in the group either getting married or having more children or moving across the country to new locations or a combination of the three. At Zion I remember the terrain changing so drastically over the course of our three days that it felt as if we were walking through an entirely new park every 5 hours or so. Some parts of the hike looked and felt like what I imagine a rain forest to be like, some areas had the dryness and wind-conditions that more closely resembled a desert, and some of it felt just like the sparse woods I encountered at Baugo Creek in Indiana where I grew up. We made the gut-wrenching journey to the edge of Angels Landing with the assistance of guide ropes, we caught a distant glimpse of The Narrows along the Virgin River, and overall just had a phenomenal time together exploring the park in such perfect weather conditions.

This trip was also unique because we made the last-second decision to spend our final night in Las Vegas together, where I tried to explain that as a tired father of three very young kids at the time and someone who consistently wore pleated khaki pants even in summer I didn't quite consider myself as the prime candidate to be allowed at the Cosmopolitan Hotel Rooftop Pool, but my friends slipped the gatekeeper a little extra money to get me in and we spent a glorious sunny afternoon having drinks and talking about all the awesome things we'd just experienced while hiking throughout Zion.

In 2016 we gathered together again to hike a massive loop throughout Rocky Mountain National Park, located just 90 minutes from Denver and situated between the small towns of Estes Park and Grand Lake. We experienced a bit more rain on this hike than we'd had on others, but we came prepared with enough ponchos and gear to make it through relatively unscathed. One of the most memorable parts of this trip was seeing the Continental Divide, which stretches from the Bering Strait above the northwestern tip of Alaska down through the Strait of Magellan in South America. In the Southern California section, water on one side of the Great Divide flows out to the Gulf of Mexico, and other side out to the Pacific Ocean. We saw several moose and deer roaming around on this adventure, witnessed one of the biggest and brightest full moons any of us had seen while hanging out after dinner one evening, and, sadly, came across a few large forest areas that were completely ravaged by a combination of the worsening bark beetle infestation that's poisoned and killed hundreds of thousands of trees and damage from a wildfire that had spread across the park a year or two prior to our arrival.

We remember the trip to Rocky Mountain National Park fondly for many reasons, but most of all we remember it because it was the last one any of us took with our friend Joe Giljum, who died in a car accident in August of the following year at the age of 36. Joe was with me during my first hike to Mount Langley in 2007 and was part of dozens of backpacking adventures with this group that spanned 20 years. His passion for the outdoors and for these trips were unmatched and all of us were devastated when we heard the awful news come across that he was gone that next summer.

In 2017 we reconvened in Joe's honor and took a trip out to Durango, Colorado with the goal of hiking the Chicago Basin trail within the Weminuche Wilderness to set up a basecamp and summit three different fourteeners over a three-day stretch. One person in our group that year had already summited 41 of the 58 fourteeners that are in the state of Colorado, and he was eager to check the box on three more beauties in a single trip on his way toward completing them all. The Chicago Basin is near a town called Silverton, and the trailhead is accessible only by train, which ended up being the best part this trip for me. The Durango & Silverton Narrow Gauge Railway is an American treasure and has been voted the best scenic train by multiple publications. After experiencing the 2.5-hour ride from the town of Durango to the Needleton stop, you quickly agree. This train began service in 1882 and is a coal-fired, steam-powered locomotive that winds through the canyons, hugging the San Juan National Forest, and provides aerial views of the 2-million-acre wilderness that are simply unmatchable. It felt like a journey back in time being on such a well-maintained style of transportation from the 1880s, and whether you were on there just for sightseeing purposes or using it to get to your trailhead as we were, everyone silently acknowledged how special it was that this train and the area around it exists in the perfect way it has for 150 years.

After we stepped off the train and got our packs settled, our hiking journey began. From the jump I could tell this would not be one of my best efforts. Everything felt off, but I couldn't pinpoint one specific thing. It started raining pretty shortly into our hike, which was not an unusual occurrence or something we hadn't dealt with before, but what was different this time was that my entire pack and all of the contents within it were getting completely soaked and I was naively unaware because I was positioned at the back of our walking line and no one was able to tell me that the protective bag I was using failed to do anything effective in keeping the elements out. Sopping wet cold clothes do not magically dry on hikes like this, especially when overnight temperatures drop to near freezing and sleeting rain continues to come down throughout the evening like it did on that first night. When the second morning began early, and the group was getting ready to head out to tackle a few of the fourteeners we'd targeted, I knew I didn't have it in me for some reason, but I gave it my best. I got 45 minutes into what would be a 10-hour day on the trails and began throwing up violently and repeatedly until I told the guys to go on without me. I was experiencing altitude sickness for the first time, and just typing the words out on the keyboard makes me feel it all over again even though it's been 4–5 years since it happened.

The remainder of that day and most of the third day was more of the same for me, unfortunately. I couldn't eat. I couldn't sleep. My clothes were drenched. And I couldn't go more than a couple hours without puking all over the place. But despite all that misery, this trip was still an amazing experience because I was going through all of this at the Chicago Basin and not anywhere else in the world. This place was magical, and the guys I was with couldn't have been more helpful and understanding about what I was dealing with, since each of them had their own stories about altitude sickness cutting them off at the knees during other hikes they'd taken. They summitted three fourteeners on that trip and came back to the campsite with all kinds of stories and exciting reports that I was thrilled they could experience. I hope I can bring my kids back to this place in the years to come and take on the three fourteeners via the Chicago Basin and accomplish the goal I happened to come a bit short on during that trip.

In one of those beautiful displays of happenstance that we are still grateful for, we came across a couple other hikers who were doing the same fourteeners that we were doing that week and ended up spending a ton of time with them. We couldn't believe it at first, but one of the guys in their group looked, sounded, and had every single physical mannerism that our recently departed friend Joe Giljum had—and those of us who knew Joe well could not stop staring at him whenever we were together.

"Holy shit," Chris said to Allen when he pulled him to the side. "That dude is literally Joe Giljum. He's a bit nicer to me than Joe was, sure—but still. Close your eyes and listen to him speak and tell me Joe isn't sitting right next to us." We loved hanging out with this guy because he was an extraordinarily strong, capable hiker who knew his stuff and was a true outdoorsman—but he had no idea the other reason we appreciated his presence so much given what happened to Joe just a couple weeks prior, and all of us were incredibly appreciative for it.

The Midwest isn't exactly known for its hiking opportunities compared with places like Colorado or Utah or Oregon, but it's no slouch when you dig deep enough and discover that it offers up some incredible places to explore once you commit yourself to finding an outdoor adventure in the area. We've taken the kids to Starved Rock State Park, Indiana Dunes National Park, the Morton Arboretum, Herrick Trail, the Prairie Path and many other large parks similar to these dozens of times collectively over the past decade and are always impressed that there are such fun and beautiful adventures to be had in an area that might as well be a direct Latin translation for "The Land of No Elevation Gains."

Anais Nin was a Cuban author who rose to prominence in America in the 1950s after spending a large portion of her life in Spain and France. Of the many quotes she's now remembered for, one of my favorites is "Each friend represents a world in us, a world possibly not born until they arrive, and it is only by this meeting that a new world is born."

There is no chance that I would be as appreciative of the outdoors as I am today or would have had such fun hiking adventures without the influence provided by Chris Chandler, Allen Narkiewicz, Joe

Giljum, and Cuyler Robinson. They opened this entire world up for me, which has added so much to my life by extension and created something so wonderful that my wife and kids now enjoy alongside me too. The backyard campouts we put on as a family each summer are one of the best days of the year where we cook on the Jet Boil and sleep in tents and hang out with flashlights under the stars. In 2018 Colleen and I knocked out our first all-day hike together when we summited Mount Quandary, a fourteener located in Breckenridge, Colorado, and had the time of our lives.

Go Find an Adventure. Enjoy it with good friends. It's always worth it.

CHAPTER 6

WORKING PARENTS FOR THE WIN

Being a dedicated parent and raising a family that you care about immensely can be an incredibly difficult endeavor to navigate.

Being a dedicated professional and having a career that you care immensely about can be an incredibly difficult endeavor to navigate.

But somehow, in one of those beautiful and miraculous twists of fate that the rich pageant of life provides its participants, taking on both things at the same time is like, *suuuuuper easy*. And what makes it even easier is when *both* parents work full-time jobs.

It's like in algebra, when the negatives across an equation cancel each other out or something like that and you're left with only the positives? I'm not sure. I didn't fare tremendously well in algebra. But you get the gist. Voila! Easy!

(End of Chapter.)

Wait hang on, what's that?

That's not an accurate description for working parents or even close to how algebra works?

Oh. Ok.

So, what I am hearing, is it turns out that the whole thing can be a little harder than "super easy" and I shouldn't even make a joke about it?

Cool. Cool cool cool.

Working parents have some strong feelings on this topic…

I have immense respect for the all the professionals out there who are putting forth their best efforts to grow and excel in their careers and are making great things happen for the teams and communities they serve. I also have immense respect for all the parents out there who are devoted to their families and spend their time and energy doing their best to cultivate a loving and supportive environment in which their children grow and flourish. For the past 11 years, Colleen and I have been taking on both meaningful tasks at the same time, like millions of other people, and have found it to be an exciting and difficult and valuable and difficult and rewarding experience. Did I say difficult?

We agree that it would be ideal if there were a scenario in which I generated enough income on my own to support our family without her having to work, so Colleen could focus exclusively on being even more present for our kids, as she wants to be. With the skyrocketing costs associated with raising five children, however, we haven't found a good way to continue providing the schooling and sports leagues and housing and orthodontics and occasional vacations our family values with only one income while still trying to save for college and retirement. Colleen was working when we met and has continued to do so, even when we had fewer than 5 kids. I have always worked full-time, and since having kids a portion of Colleen's work has been part-time employment and some of it has been full-time employment, but it's always been part of our lives as parents and something we've all worked together on to balance and keep alignment on as we progressed. Overall, we feel this setup has worked out extremely well for our entire family for a variety of reasons.

Colleen is a powerhouse when it comes to her career, and I love that our kids get to see her perform in a professional setting, so they have such a great role model if they end up following a similar path. She graduated near the top of her class at a very competitive high school and received an undergrad degree in Accounting from the University of Illinois, which was one of the best accountancy programs in the nation at the time. She then got a Master's Degree in Accountancy from the same program and later earned her CPA license. She's worked as a broker and consultant in the Employee Benefits Insurance industry for 20 years and has been a rockstar each step of the way. I am so grateful that our kids get to see this kind of achievement and excellence in the comprehensive way they do so they know the hard work it takes to be successful and can feel proud that their mom is such a capable and competent businesswoman and leader—all while being the most dedicated, supporting, loving, and hands-on mother to her kids.

We think it's been extremely valuable that our kids have witnessed both of their parents excel, struggle, win, lose, lead, fail, and accomplish milestones in their careers because it's opening their eyes and minds to become more confident pursuing whatever careers or professions they will eventually step into as they get older. The kids get to celebrate with us when great things happen at work, and they learn from us how to properly react when difficult situations arise in our jobs. They get to champion Colleen when she leads one of the biggest conferences of her career in flawless fashion and they see how much time and effort she puts forth to be great at what she does. They see me taking calls at all hours of the day and night, they see me working long after I have put them to bed to catch up on some of the projects that might have gotten delayed because I was able to volunteer at recess at school during the day, and they see me traveling across the country to support my team and partners whenever necessary.

They see us fulfilling our commitments to our jobs and most importantly doing so without compromising any of the deeper covenants we have to our family. They have seen from the very beginning that at no point have Colleen or I had to truly sacrifice any of their critical needs or lessen our commitment to them while raising our family and working. We are there when they get on the bus to start their day, we are there when they return home to get going with snack time and homework, and we can volunteer at their school and participate in parent groups like any other family.

Are we able to make every single school volunteer event? Nope. Are we able to commit to joining as many midday group-workout sessions or coffee breaks with our friends that have a little more free time and flexibility than we have? Not even close. Has one of us had to miss the occasional soccer game or volleyball event or neighborhood social function with the kids due to being out of town? You betcha. But we're there when the kids need us, and they understand the "why" behind both of us working, which is always focused around creating more opportunities and a good path for our entire family.

Of course, there are plenty of moments filled with extreme chaos where the balance between working and parenting can get more out of sync than any of us would prefer, and it feels as if everyone's hair is on fire. And in the summer? Forget about it. That's an entirely different animal for which there is no cage. Whether you have 1 kid or 8 kids, 2 working parents or 1 working parent or 0 working parents, summer is a humbling and exhausting marathon for every parent out there trying their best to make it a fun, safe, and memorable experience for their family. Even with the "Minivan Mafia" community of parents we have around our town that assist with carpooling and jumping in to help each other whenever it is needed, it is a vastly steep challenge to perform professional responsibilities and ensure you're getting every kid to every activity on time while keeping them fed in a healthy fashion and fully caked in enough sunscreen to add 4–5 pounds to their overall body weight.

And after the sunscreen has been applied it turns out you didn't pack a water bottle, or you made a mistake on what was prepared for lunch because you forgot peanut butter caused allergy concerns at camp, so you have to turn around and start again. Then you went accidentally drove another child to the wrong field to drop them off for practice because there is one starting right after it in a different place across the city that you got confused with. You did this while on an important work call knowing that when it is complete you need to pick up your son and four neighborhood kids from the swimming lessons that have been waiting on you for 15 minutes because you're running very late and you still haven't eaten breakfast or combed your hair. And it's still somehow only 9:15 a.m., with about 11 more activities to get through that day. This is not to say we are complaining about any of it, either. There is no martyrdom here. But it is quite a bit to manage and that's just what we do…some days more effectively than others.

Everyone had it hard during the pandemic and there is no "ranking" of who had it the toughest. In many ways the experience was the ultimate equalizer…there was no amount of wealth or social status that could keep you sheltered from the impact of isolation, fear, uncertainty, and disruption of life that everyone encountered in one way or another from March 2020 through COVID. Parents, non-parents, married, single, woman, man, young, old, professionals, unemployed—everyone felt it in some way and it altered life as we knew it for all of us.

That said, there was a shift that came about during the pandemic that provided exposure to what working parents were dealing with that gave others a peek into just how challenging this situation was for them and their children to endure.

In addition to the uncertainty of how they would adapt to performing their professional jobs from home when their makeshift workspace was not prepared to do so and learning how on Earth they were going to run Ops meetings from their kitchen, working parents were tasked with taking on an entirely different full-time responsibility for which most were wildly unqualified to perform. They were Mom and Dad and remained Mom and Dad, but now they were Teacher. Now they were Indoor Recess Monitor. Now they were Cafeteria Assistant. Now they were Principal, Vice Principal, Janitor, Librarian, and every other important position that influences children at their school, because all of that went away overnight and was placed in the laps of working parents to deal with exclusively. All of this while working parents were worrying about their own job security and trying to keep their professional ship afloat and praying to remain employed during one of the worst social and economic crises anyone alive had experienced hoping they could still support their families in such a challenging time.

And if their professional jobs ever felt somewhat stable, working parents' concern would shift immediately back to their kids' well-being and how all these changes were impacting their development. Working parents have a level of consistent, underlying guilt that is always present, no matter how good of a job they do at hitting the work/life balance or how well-adjusted their kids are. It's always there; sometimes in big ways that overwhelm you, and sometimes in diminutive ways that you almost forget about, but it's there. When schools were shut down due to COVID, the guilt was close to an all-time high for most working parents, because there wasn't much they could do to make this situation any better for children who were clearly struggling to learn virtually, or stay attentive during class, or understand challenging school subjects without the kind of guidance and instruction they were used to. Parents felt they were failing at their jobs, and they felt as if they were failing at home. It's a common and less than ideal feeling, but one that was made exponentially larger throughout the pandemic.

And people like Colleen and I were actually pretty lucky. This ordeal was far, far worse for those working parents who were healthcare workers, first responders, fast-food workers, store cashiers, manufacturing crews, or other essential workers who had to go into the hospital/plant/supermarket to perform their jobs without knowing how their childcare and schooling situation was going to be taken care of.

But what ended up happening as time and instability and fear continued to progress? Did families and schools and the broader society at large collapse? No. Working parents answered the bell, just as they always do. It took some time, but eventually people started developing different expectations and schedules that made way more sense than those that we attempted at the beginning of the lockdown. Working parents came up with new routines that worked for their jobs and for their kids; it just so happened that it all took place under the same roof with no one ever leaving the house this time around.

And in another incredible development that was clearly a result of the pandemic, many of the non-parent professionals became the best kind of allies possible. All professionals got to show more of themselves to each other at work…we met your children, your spouses, your pets, your roommates, we saw your bedrooms and living rooms and we heard your landscapers blowing your leaves across your yard. Colleagues and managers become much more understanding when employees without kids needed a mental break to reset and take better care of themselves, and they showed the same kind of grace when working parents needed to step away to perform Mom/Dad duties that required their full attention, even if it happened to be during the workday. We all started working better together, and understanding each other better, and having more empathy toward each other. We knew that whatever situation you were dealing with, it was a lot, and required us to be a bit more kind and caring toward each other than we may have been in the past. I don't think this improved trend is going to go away for a very long time, and I think all of us—working parents, non-working parents, non-parent professionals, the companies and families we work for—are much better off because of it.

Our kids have been in every kind of daycare facility possible throughout Colleen's and my careers. Big ones, small ones, new ones, old ones, ones inside a house, ones within a strip mall—you name it. We've been exposed to every kind of sinus infection and head cold and every variation of the hand, foot, and mouth disease out there. Our kids' immune systems were made stronger from all these facilities, but more importantly, we believe our kids' development was made stronger in so many great ways from all these facilities. We're grateful for all the people who have helped them get ready for school at these places and the awesome friends they made along the way.

Most people you encounter are doing the best they can when they're feeling right in their hearts and minds. Their best is different on different days, and I've learned that everyone is carrying a ton of weight within them, whether you can see it or not. I am not going to suggest that working parents are carrying the most weight—as if it's a competition of some sort—but they're usually carrying two very important pieces of their lives at one time trying to serve both in the best possible fashion. They are doing so with the knowledge that when one of them falls out of sync, it can drastically impact the other. Those working parents out there who provide for their children and are committed to being the best possible role models—even at times that are less than perfect—are splendid examples for children to learn from and have my utmost respect for doing whatever it takes to create a better life for their families.

CHAPTER 7

I THINK DAVID FOSTER WALLACE WAS RIGHT

I first came across the work of David Foster Wallace in a manner that he would likely be extremely disappointed to learn.

Despite the fact that Wallace is one of Americas most celebrated authors—his enduring masterpiece, *Infinite Jest* is widely considered one of the great novels of the 20th century—I had never heard of him until scrolling through YouTube a few years ago and noticing a commencement speech with the title "This Is Water," which I thought sounded interesting enough to give a listen.

For a writer as prolific and insightful as Wallace was, getting noticed online and lauded for a *commencement speech* might be something he would have considered to be about as unpoetically cruel justice as it gets. But that's how I stumbled upon him and I'm positive there are plenty others like me out there given how popular that speech has become since it was delivered at Kenyon College in the spring of 2005.

The 23-minute speech showcases Wallace identifying a wildly difficult problem to even *recognize* in our everyday lives, which is impressive enough. He then goes on to figure out a solution to this problem and shares deep ways we can improve the quality and meaningfulness of our very existence. That's quite an undertaking for any serious thinker to ponder, let alone articulate to the world in a clearly understandable fashion in a commencement speech forum.

The theme of his speech is the value an education should provide. Wallace posits that an education has less to do with specific knowledge than it does having a heightened sense of awareness—awareness of what is around us but hidden in plain sight, awareness that we have the ability and responsibility to choose superior methods of thinking within the everyday situations we so frequently find ourselves in other than the problematic "default settings" that accompany the day-in-and day-out-routines that modern professional adult life entails.

The part of the speech that struck me most when I first heard it—and the part I try to keep at the front of my mind most often—is around the choices we make when it comes to what we worship and how we can unconsciously choose paths that lead toward self-destruction despite the influence that society has in telling us those are the values and ideas that should be vigorously pursued.

Wallace was not taking the pulpit that day as some dogmatic preacher speaking on behalf of religious texts. He was raised by staunch atheists and considered himself an atheist publicly for a long time. He was eventually tabbed as agnostic, and whether that's an accurate depiction of how he truly felt doesn't matter except to convey that this speech was coming from someone who was at the very least deeply skeptical about the ideas of God and religion being relied on as fundamental truths.

When the notion of worship came up in the speech, however, Wallace made the bold assertion that there is no *such thing* as atheism in our world. There is no such thing as *not worshipping*. Everyone is worshipping *something*; the only choice we get is *what* to worship.

Wallace didn't appear convinced in the idea of God the way that it is represented in a variety of popular global religions, but from a practical perspective he went on to state that he believed there were very compelling reasons to choose a God or a religion or spiritual figure or a set of inviolable ethical principles to worship instead of any alternative—and his reasoning was that compared with God and religion "pretty much anything else you worship will eat you alive."

He went on to give specific examples of things people worship and what the risk is in putting your time, effort, faith, and worship into that idea or practice.

"If you worship money and things, if they are where you tap real meaning in life, then you will never feel like you have enough."

"If you worship your own body and beauty and sexual allure, you will always feel ugly. And when time and age start showing, you will die a million deaths before they finally plant you."

"If you worship power, you will end up feeling weak and afraid—and you will need ever more power over others to numb you to your own fear."

"If you worship your intellect, being seen as smart—you will end up feeling stupid, a fraud, always on the verge of being found out."

Wallace explained that these particular areas of worship are not evil or sinful in and of themselves—the scariest part about them is that they are most often unconscious, a default setting that you gradually slip into without being aware that's where you're deriving your value from in life, which inevitably leads toward destruction over time. I found all of that so captivating when I first heard it because somewhere, I knew all of it to be true and familiar but had never had it broken down and explained so clearly. This was a revelation to me, but of something I'd already known.

I started to connect these ideas to what I'd studied previously when trying to better understand the Seven Deadly Sins. One of the most fascinating things I came across when diving into them was that each of the Seven Deadly Sins (or Vices) had a Cardinal Virtue that coincided with it and worked as a counteragent—again, something that made instant sense when I thought about it and knew it to be true, but hadn't fully considered before in those terms.

The first thoughts or emotions I tend to experience in my default setting when dealing with difficult situations often lean more toward the Seven Deadly Sins column than the column of Virtues...I have to actively recognize those feelings, understand that they wouldn't serve me or my community in the best way, and actively choose to instead act in a manner that more closely resembles the corresponding Virtue. I also noticed that whenever my life seems out of balance or in a bad place, I can usually point to one of the Seven Deadly Sins that is looming larger over my mind and existence than it should and is causing the unsettledness and negative feelings I'm experiencing. When it works properly, it's the *awareness* of that negative mindset that Wallace describes that allows me to then *choose* a better way.

- When I would take part in acts of *Gluttony*, being excessive in food or drink, I would have to choose instead to live with *Temperance,* moderation and voluntary self-restraint.
- When I would feel *Greed* coming on, the excessive desire for material things taking over my heart, I would have to choose instead to act with *Charity,* voluntarily helping those in need and seeing my neighbor as I see myself.
- When I would feel *Lust*, inordinate craving for pleasures of the body, I would have to choose instead to act with *Chastity,* refraining from physical activity considered immoral.
- When I would limit my activities to the point of *Sloth*, the avoidance of physical or spiritual work, I would have to choose instead to act with *Diligence,* the act of carefulness and persistent effort of work.
- When I would feel *Wrath* take over, uncontrollable anger or hatred, I would have to choose instead to act with *Patience*, the ability to wait for something without frustration as well as with *Forgiveness.*
- When I would feel *Envy*, that awful sense of jealousy or sadness about someone else's goods or situation, I would

have to choose instead to act with *Kindness,* showing love and being a sympathetic, considerate person.

• When I would feel *Pride,* living life centered on myself and excessive belief in my own abilities, I would have to choose instead to act with *Humility,* recognizing that we need each other, that I am not the center of the universe, that I have more to learn, and operating with the freedom from arrogance.

I am a practicing Catholic and someone who values organized religion. That doesn't mean I think organized religion is perfect and it doesn't mean the application of my faith has been anywhere near perfect. But I've felt the benefits of having been part of this type of religious community and believe it has helped me live a better and more meaningful life than what I would have without it. I believe the virtues and ideals that are extolled in most religions are worthy of worship because it helps people determine a more positive aim and principles by which to live. Even if I weren't religious, I would think that I could look at each of these Seven Deadly Sins and conclude that by acting in that particular manner they would lead me down a less optimal path for myself and others than the one I would walk on if I chose instead to follow the seven corresponding virtues.

I don't have to agree with everything he wrote, or thought, or even necessarily the way he lived in his life—but I think David Foster Wallace was right when it comes to the message he crafted and shared in his speech "This is Water." Becoming aware of your situation and mindset and taking on the responsibility to choose the way you interpret the world is better than the alternative of living by the unconscious default settings and negative knee-jerk reactions that tend to come through in our minds during the day-in and day-out existence of our lives leading us away from an undeniably superior way to operate.

You can make that mundane trip to the grocery store better and more meaningful. You can make that interaction with a stranger or loved one better and more meaningful. You can make that traffic jam better and more meaningful. It's not easy, but the real value to be unlocked through a worthwhile education teaches you that it's possible and that it's up to you to make it happen.

CHAPTER 8

AUGUST 31, 2008

Not every day you go through will end up completely altering the overall trajectory of your life in ways you're able to fully recognize and understand. But every single day has the *potential* to. And I know that, because for me August 31, 2008, was the day I can point to with absolute certainty, knowing that every part of my life was changed from that point forward, and changed for the best.

The morning started in rather unremarkable fashion with me waking up tired and searching for coffee after a night out in the city with friends. I was playing rugby at the time for the Chicago Lions. We'd just completed a highly successful Summer 7's campaign in which we'd torn through the regular season qualifiers in May and June—eventually winning the Division 1 Men's Midwest Championships in July—and finished sixth at the National Championship event held at Treasure Island in San Francisco a couple weeks earlier. August 31st was the Sunday of a long Labor Day weekend, and my teammates and I had spent Friday and Saturday night getting some good old-fashioned fun in before the fall training sessions picked up again full time in September.

On this Sunday morning, however, I was not interested in any more fun. I'd had it already. I was out too late Friday night, and I was out too late Saturday night. This Sunday, I told myself, would be "Dennis Improvement Day." No more messing around. No more enjoyment of cold beers and frolicking in the sunshine in the best city in the world—nope, not today. This Sunday I would be focused on far more productive activities like rigorous exercise, reading long Russian novels, writing original poetry, calling my grandmother to check in, volunteering at animal shelters, and eating only the healthiest of fare to energize the battered temple that was my body. I'd spent too much time going out already that weekend; this day would be a day of Stoicism the likes of which would make Marcus Aurelius blush, and it would begin with a challenging 30-mile bike ride in the blazing heat near the lakeshore to get myself right.

The plan I developed for that day had real gusto, but it didn't get very far compared with what actually happened. I made it exactly two city blocks to the corner of Clark and Addison on this *bike ride of tremendous expectation*s when I heard a couple familiar voices scream out, "O'Donnell!! Hey, you sonofabitch let's go!! Pub is this way and the Cubs game starts in an hour!!" It was two teammates of mine, and they were considerably more awake and thirstier than I was at 11:30 a.m. One of these friends hailed from Ireland originally, the other was from England, and neither of them were in the mood to be told "no" by some 25-year-old American with shoulder-length hair who was getting started with a day that was inspired by a combination of Richard Simmons and Tony Robbins.

"One drink—*one drink*, guys. Then I am off. I've got a ton I have to get done today. Seriously. Just one, OK?" was the best response I could muster in the face of these two very persuasive international ruggers who were looking for another wingman. We walked together down to a bar called Casey Moran's right outside Wrigley Field, where I parked my bike and proceeded to make my way inside wearing gym shorts and a cutoff tee shirt.

I was just a few hours into "Dennis Improvement Day," and it was turning out to be pretty similar to what had taken place throughout the previous two nights. The three of us were having a blast together enjoying the rooftop at Casey Moran's and eventually made our way down to the first floor to post up near the bar, where we watched hopeful Phillies fans pour in before the first pitch trying to soak up as much of the Wrigleyville experience as they could while in town visiting. The game eventually started and those inside the bar with tickets excitedly strolled across the street into the most beautiful baseball field our country has to offer to watch their beloved team play on a gorgeous, clear-skied afternoon.

Serendipitously enough, however, there was one group of girls we noticed who were not able to find tickets to the game that day, who had made their way from Wrigley Field over to Casey Moran's to watch the game on television instead. My two friends thought this development was remarkable—and by that word, I mean they were literally unable to not make remarks as soon as they saw the group walk in.

"Wow, look at you in that dress. What are you drinking? I'm buying!" the one from Ireland said loudly and full of confidence.

As someone born and raised in Indiana, with no accent or brogue or dialect of any interest at all to anyone ever, I watched and listened to this brash comment being said and fully expected the group of girls he was talking at to either completely ignore him or slap him across his face. I know for a 10,000 percent fact that had I said that exact phrase to anyone, especially a group of women that were so put together and strong and capable, that would have been the result because I sound like I sound when I speak, and I do not sound like he sounded when he spoke.

But not only did the group of women *not* run away or slap my self-assured friend, they laughed—loudly—and walked right past me over to his shoulder where they immediately struck up a bristling conversation that was full of light banter. I did not see that result coming.

And the only part that surprised me more, was when my friend from England started talking and the same thing happened to him.

Eventually the prettiest girl in the bunch made her way over near me and didn't seem disappointed to hear that I had a Midwestern accent, which I took as a pretty positive sign. We talked together pretty much by ourselves away from our groups of friends for hours that afternoon as I tried like hell to get her to start liking me as much as I knew I liked her the second we met. She had the most radiant smile I'd ever seen and every part of our conversation that day felt fun and carefree, but also intimate somehow, even though we'd just met. She was quick-witted and kind. She was discerning. She had a confident humility about her. Her long blonde hair and deep green eyes were a marvel to me, and I couldn't take my gaze away from her. She was an absolute knockout.

It took a few weeks after that first chance encounter, but eventually we started dating exclusively and when it started, we both had a very, very good feeling that it was different and better and "more" than anything we'd experienced before.

She very quickly became the person I wanted to spend the most time with, and it wasn't even close. We started spending every available part of the day together. We would get together right after work and walk around the city for hours—sometimes we'd stop by friends' houses to hang out, other times we would just walk by ourselves around Old Town or Gold Coast or Wicker Park or Lakeview or anywhere else and gaze at the beautiful city we lived in and loved so much together. We'd go to restaurants, parks, movies, or sit around together and do nothing at all —it didn't matter; if we were together, we were happy. I still played for the Chicago Lions, but it started falling down the list of priorities and was replaced with getting to know everything I could about Colleen, her family, her friends—I wanted to do anything I could to get closer with her, and it felt as if there was never a second wasted while I was in her presence.

We had our first date at Om on the Range yoga studio in the Ravenswood neighborhood in September 2008, we exchanged our first "I Love You's" in December 2008, we dated for a year before I asked her to marry me in November 2009, and we were married six months later in April 2010. Our first child was born in February 2011 and from there we proceeded to move five times and welcome four more amazing children into this world over the course of just six years on the journey of a lifetime.

It's impossible to express all the ways I am impressed by Colleen as a human being and admire her, but I'll provide a couple.

When she is your friend, there is simply no one better in the world to have in your corner. She is supportive, she's an outstanding listener, and she is fiercely loyal—even when you're wrong, she will kindly try to guide you closer to the right direction, all while making you feel seen and heard for the wild ideas you're thinking through at the time. She doesn't gossip, she doesn't speak ill of others unnecessarily, and she doesn't see value in pretending to be something she isn't when different groups of people are around her.

There are children in this world right now that she did not give birth to that may not be here if it wasn't for Colleen…she has lent her ear to so many women considering having children, considering having more children, etc., and Colleen is always there to provide encouragement and love to give them confidence each step throughout what is usually a quite vulnerable and challenging discussion for someone to engage in. It's beautiful to see.

She is the queen of all holiday decorations. I love this because it so clearly showcases the spirit and enthusiasm she has for life and for celebrating being alive. Christmas, Easter, Arbor Day, Thanksgiving, Halloween, Flag Day…they all get the same treatment around our house, and they're all given special attention, which makes our home a warmer and more vibrant and fun and lively place to be for our family and friends.

She is ethical—so much so, in fact, that she gets visibly angry even when people in movies or TV shows lie and steal or do awful things to each other. Her morals are incredibly strong, and she does the right thing in so many situations, even when no one is paying attention and she has the opportunity to perform a self-serving act that no one would ever find out about.

She is smart and incredibly capable: she obtained an undergrad accounting degree from the University of Illinois, which was the number one ranked school for that major in the country at that time. From there she went on to get a Master's in Accountancy and eventually earned a CPA license. She now works full time while raising five kids and leads a team that is changing the way the insurance industry executes its wellness plans, and she is the one helping steer the ship. Not one part of that is easy or able to be accomplished without a ridiculous amount of competency, drive, grit, and intelligence.

She puts so much effort into being the best mother she can possibly be to her children. When you watch her in action, it's like watching a fish swim, everything appears to come so naturally to her. But she is also constantly learning and shifting her approach to apply to whatever emotions are being felt that particular day or when one of our children pass through another developmental phase altogether, which requires a diverse set of tools to work with. No matter what the situation calls for, she shows up 10,000 percent for her children in every way and provides the type of unconditional love and security and kindness to them that could only come from her.

I remember a lyric from the Led Zeppelin song "Going to California" that I thought about often as I was working on improving myself and dating various people over time while living downtown before meeting Colleen. The more people I met and dated, the more it became clear that I had quite a few qualities and traits and habits that needed work, because some of the people I was attracting didn't fit the vision of the type of person I would look for in a lifelong partnership. I am firm believer in the idea that you will attract the type of energy and emotions that you put out into the universe.

The lyric went:

"Find a queen without a king
They say she plays guitar and cries and sings
Ride a white mare in the footsteps of dawn
Tryin' to find a woman who's never, never, never been born"

It was the last line of that lyric that stayed with me...were my standards too high? Did a woman like the one I envisioned even exist? Could someone out there be kind, and funny, and smart, and driven, and caring, and beautiful, with a set of moral and ethical standards that I respected and admired?

When I met Colleen, I was far, far short of being the caliber of person that I thought she deserved, but she saw something in me and gave me a chance and she has helped make be a better person every step of the way since that time.

I also knew that when I met Colleen, I finally knew the answer to the question I thought about from the "Going to California" lyric—it turns out a person like this did exist, she had been born, and I was grateful that the prayers I prayed had allowed me to find her.

And so...August 31, 2008, turned out to be a "Dennis Improvement Day" after all.

CHAPTER 9

I LOVE WATCHING YOU PLAY

We are blessed to have five active, healthy, athletic kids that love playing sports. Basketball, soccer, lacrosse, volleyball, swimming, softball—you name it, they're into it, and we do the best we can to get them exposed to whatever activities they have an interest in. Most of these sports have seasons that overlap with each other, which means our kids can have two or more commitments that are going on at the same time, which also means we can have anywhere between 8 and 15 games and practices across our family on any given weekend when these sports are in full swing. This can be quite a bit to undertake when you're driving and watching all the events you're trying to get to and still making time for birthday parties, family time, and just good ol' fashioned downtime where nothing at all is scheduled.

Given how much time we've spent watching so many games over the years, I can unequivocally state that there is no shortage of crazy sports parents out there right now, and they seem to multiply like gremlins with each new season. I'm not sure if there is something in the protein shakes that's driving this insane behavior or if parents feel that the scouts for the NBA, MLS, NHL, and Olympics are super interested in attending their 7 year old's games, but some of these people are just not doing a solid service to their kids when they act the way they do on the sidelines. It's tough to watch.

Most parents we've come across are good, supportive spectators. They cheer on their son or daughter; they root for their team and provide positive feedback; they refrain from criticizing the referees, coaches, and opponents on the field (at least not loud enough for anyone on the field to hear); and they accept that they're watching young kids play a game that is supposed to be framed around having fun.

This is the sort of thing that tends to work out pretty well for everyone involved.

But then…there are some others. They're the ones that accuse their kid (or even worse, other kids) of not hustling enough during game-play—loudly enough for everyone to hear, embarrassing him or her in front of their friends. They berate the referee for missing a foul call, even though it's obvious that he's a volunteer—or not getting paid a ton of money—and clearly doesn't have a stake in the outcome of the game. They peacock around the sidelines and only seem to have negative things to say to the players and spectators around them, because nothing is living up to the wild and unrealistic and strange expectations they have for what's going on around them.

I can't tell you how many kids we've seen come off the field or the court that look like the last thing they want to do is get into that car with their parents whom they just heard screaming at them the entire game, because they know they're about to catch an earful about their performance.

This is the sort of thing that tends to work out pretty poorly for everyone involved.

A couple years ago I listened to a Ted Talk from a former professional soccer coach named John O'Sullivan who has made it his mission to create positive changes in youth sports in America. John started a company that works with coaches and youth sports leagues across the country with the goal of "giving youth sports back to kids" and creating an environment that is based on having fun instead of churning out extremely high performers and burning kids out to the point they exit playing sports altogether at a very young age. During this talk he delivered a catchphrase that I have tried to remember every time I attend one of my kids' events or am having a conversation with them about their performance. It consists of just 5 words, and it changes everything:

"I Love Watching You Play."

That's it. When kids hear that phrase from their parents, instead of getting criticized for their play, they feel safe and cared for and they have a better chance at experiencing the fun that the game is supposed to have for them. Kids crave love and support from their parents. None of that should be conditional on how they played as a goalie or how many three-pointers they made or whether they won or lost or how they performed at all.

I learned that the more often I said this phrase to my kids, the more it became true. I started to watch their games with a different lens—one of gratitude that I had a child who was capable and healthy enough to play youth sports and appeared to be having a great time while doing so. I appreciated their performance, knowing that what they're doing isn't easy, and to them could feel like Game 7 of the World Series. They didn't need anyone else trying to make the stage bigger for them.

Are there times I slip up and get frustrated if one of my kids has a bad attitude during the game? Sure, everyone does. But when you come back to the phrase "I love watching you play," all the negativity and weight and room for criticism vanishes. Which turns out to be the sort of thing that tends to work out pretty well for everyone involved.

The lessons sports can teach kids are invaluable. We want our kids to be competitive. We want them to play hard. We want them to struggle out there from time to time so they know how to handle adversity and pressure. But much more than that, we want them to demonstrate great teamwork and to be a good sport to their opponent and to be unselfish and to have a fun time with their friends, enjoying an activity that they love playing together.

We want them to remember to always say "thank you" to the coaches and referees after a game. We want them to come home knowing that whatever happened on the field a few minutes beforehand doesn't matter as much as the privilege we have to be together in our home as a family and it has nothing to do with how anyone performed in a game.

"I love watching you play" was intended for parents as a way to mitigate their tendency to place undue pressure and fervor on the children they're watching play youth sports, but it works wonders for the kids that hear it too, and I believe it is a message worthy of being spread.

CHAPTER 10

OUTSIDE IS BETTER THAN INSIDE

This one has to be on the Top 5 list of "Most Repeated O'Donnell Family Mottos" that Colleen and I have in our repertoire. We have said this out loud nearly every day for almost ten years running. This phrase also might be the one and only bumper sticker that I could see on the back of a car and say, "I should get one of those."

Our appreciation for all things outside has only grown since having children, because we both saw very early on what an undeniably positive impact getting outdoors had on our kids' attitudes, mental outlook, physical health, and happiness. On pretty much any day when we're not in school or doing homework or completely shut in due to inclement Illinois weather you will likely find us (or at least our kids) outside around the neighborhood riding bikes, swimming, playing basketball, playing soccer, playing pickleball, playing lacrosse, playing with dogs, roller-blading, or simply taking in the vibe of being in the great outdoors. Our house is located right next to a huge park in Wheaton with acres of wide-open green grass that presents the opportunity to make an unbelievable time out of any day, with nothing required but motivation and a little creativity.

Our kids have learned that when Colleen and I walk into a room after we think they've been stuck to a television too long or spending more time than beneficial on an iPad and shout, "Outside is better than inside!" they immediately meander over to the mudroom almost unconsciously to get their socks and shoes on and head out toward the door. Their response has become Pavlovian, and it makes us smile every time it happens.

We love taking family walks around our Danada East neighborhood, walking together to get ice cream, walking together to get lunch, walking together to the movie theatre, walking together to church, walking together downtown to get a drink for date night, walking together to our friends' houses to hang out, etc. There's a pretty consistent theme there if you look closely enough.

Colleen's and my favorite state is Wisconsin, not only because of the fun and festive people that live there—who value a cold beer and delicious bratwurst as much as we do—but because most of the time we spend there happens to be outside in active ways. We usually visit a couple times a year and always have the best time enjoying the clear, crisp, beautiful area that feels as if it was just made to be explored for hours and hours on end. We are usually in the water or riding bikes or walking back and forth to town and couldn't appreciate it more. Our kids are dead tired when evening comes around, and they sleep without effort throughout the night and until late morning. Those are good days.

"But Dennis, what about when it's too cold or rainy out? Then what? Isn't inside better?"

Awesome. Get your boots, a jacket, big gloves, hat, and scarf, have an adventure and we'll see you in 20 minutes. I've learned that I always feel better even after minimal time spent outside even in terrible weather, and so do our kids.

I used to really struggle through the Midwestern winters and would spend most days staring at a calendar pinned to the month of June while artificial sunlight beaming from an electronic box bounced off my face near my desk to lift my spirits. Every day felt awful, and I rarely ventured outside in the dreary, freezing temperatures that did nothing but make me sad and angry for weeks at a time. Then our children started getting older and would ask to do fun stuff like sledding and building snowmen and having snowball fights. I wasn't going to say "no" just because I happened to be the one feeling a bit blue. Whenever we did these activities, I noticed how much better and happier I would feel, even in the worst possible weather conditions. Winter is still tough and yes, some days are just unbearably bad, but I found ways to embrace it and it was precisely through bundling up and spending more time outside. That hot chocolate with marshmallows tasted way better when I earned it with some outdoor time, too.

Colleen and I picked up sets of snowshoes and would take late night walks around the park near our house and throughout the neighborhood after our kids were in bed, and it quickly became one of our favorite things to do in the winter. I'd never even considered something like that before, but as soon as we started, we became hooked and were grateful to have found an unbelievably fun twist to make our surroundings more enjoyable in what used to be considered dreary weather.

As adults we can forget how much fun bad weather can be when you get the right gear on and brave it for a little bit. When was the last time I grabbed an umbrella and took a long walk when it was pouring outside? Not a rushed pace trying to get inside my car or back inside the office when it's raining; I mean like a real walk, with the intention of just walking, while wearing the right clothing and holding an umbrella that kept me relatively dry? When I did those kinds of activities, I noticed they were kind of fantastic, but it usually isn't the first thought that pops into your mind when you see the storm clouds rolling into town. Any weather you encounter presents an opportunity to take it on and enjoy it outside with a little creativity and bravery.

There is nothing evil or wrong or wasteful about time spent relaxing, such as watching television, being on iPads, taking in movies, or playing video games. Watching movies and taking the kids to the theater is among my favorite activities ever, and video games are flat-out *awesome*. They have provided hours of fun family time that we've thoroughly enjoyed together, and they can teach kids valuable skills like teamwork, creative problem solving, and coding. You will not find a bigger fan of Luigi's Mansion 3 on the Nintendo Switch than I am, and the memories I have from playing games like that with my kids are moments I truly treasure.

But like anything else, when too much time is spent on inside activities like TV or video games—which have become highly addictive and are developed with a few devious social engineering tricks designed to keep kids playing longer than ever before—it becomes seriously detrimental. We believe that a proper balance can be struck with time spent being active outside—no matter what your specific hobbies or interests are, there is something for everyone out there.

Outside is better than Inside. It's more than just a catchphrase around our house, and we love it.

CHAPTER 11

POCKET TENS, AS PEOPLE

My father is the best poker player anyone from the greater South Bend region has ever met. Texas Hold 'Em. Razz. Stud. Omaha. Doesn't matter which game. All the people who have lost money to him playing cards will quickly agree with this statement, and those who don't recognize him as the greatest just haven't played against him enough yet. It's that simple.

He honed his card-playing chops while bartending at an infamous watering hole called The B&B where I was born and raised in Osceola, Indiana, while he was in high school. For those of you unfamiliar with the town of Osceola, B&B did not stand for "Bed and Breakfast" or anything cute resembling that more widely known acronym. In fact, when I asked my dad what the letters in The B&B stood for as a kid, he told me it meant "The Bloody Bucket" due to the number of violent fights that would break out there during all hours of operation—and if you ever frequented this establishment in the 70's and 80's, you would know that his description is beyond 100 percent accurate.

Three other bartenders worked alongside my dad during that time. One was affectionately known as One-Eyed-Steve because, creatively enough, he had one eye and his name was Steve. Another was Wally Gator, a large, grizzled, bearded man who also had only one eye after getting the other one beaten out with a pistol during a back-alley brawl in the 70's —and also the only guy I've ever met that had an unmistakable Pabst Blue Ribbon tattoo on his forearm. Somehow, there was yet *another* bartender with one eye named Wacky Jackie, a small but fierce woman who'd racked up four DUI's and tried to make Christian-converts out of anyone around if they stayed at the bar past 1:30 a.m.

For those of you keeping score at home, that's four people bartending and a total of five eyeballs.

Each of these three bartenders were great people to me when I was a kid and always treated me extremely friendly when I was hanging around, but highlighting them here helps color in the picture of the types of activities that were taking place around The B&B and throughout Osceola at the time.

The B&B was owned by a notorious and successful local entrepreneur named Julius Werbrouck. Among the litany of legal issues Julius had been beset with over the years, he was indicted in 1977 for violating federal gambling laws at a hotel he owned, and he was connected with the closest thing the region has ever seen to a mafia. To an outsider, it would be easy to make a quick and harsh judgment on what kind of men Julius Werbrouck and his associates were. Those closest to him knew also what kind of man Julius was, but the answer differed vastly from those given by the outsiders.

Julius and my dad hit it off immediately while working together, and Julius eventually came to look after my father as if he were his son, representing the closest thing I had to a day-in-and-day-out grandfather when I was growing up. My paternal grandfather was a great family man, but he lived in California, so unfortunately I wasn't able to talk with him or see him as often as we both would have liked, and my maternal grandfather that lived near us suffered from quite a few serious physical ailments that kept him from being active in my family's life when I was growing up. So Julius filled that role for me, and I loved him just as much as I loved those who were blood relatives. My mom has told me that she never saw Julius happier than on the day she and my father got married. And on the day I was born, Julius's house was the very first place my father stopped to share the news and celebrate.

Julius came to the house regularly with gifts I cherished, like sports memorabilia and old decorations he took down from The B&B that he couldn't stand to see thrown out without checking whether I wanted them first. I remember him coming to the house to celebrate birthdays with me or to watch a football game in the garage and always making me feel as if I was the person he was most looking forward to seeing that day…it's hard to overstate how much that means to a kid sometimes.

My dad was the second oldest of eleven children born into one of those great classic Irish Catholic families. They moved from New Jersey to Indiana when he was a youth, then when he was in high school his entire family moved from Indiana to California, but he decided to live in a tent in his friend's backyard in Osceola one summer rather than follow along with them to warmer weather and oceanside views out west. Sometimes I would ask him questions like, "Man, Dad, what was it like growing up in such a big family? It had to be so much fun; I would have loved that! So many fun people around, tell me more!"

"I decided to stay here in Osceola to live in a tent instead of going to California, Dennis. What does that tell you?" And before I knew it, the conversation was over.

Most Saturday mornings when I was growing up, my dad would play poker and have a couple cocktails down at The B&B with a pretty consistent cohort of card sharks before the night crowd came through. On more than a few occasions I would accompany him to hang out away from the action to drink Pepsi and watch sports highlights from the night before and learn more about all the games that were coming up that day. My dad was no longer bartending there, but we'd ingrained ourselves so deeply with the establishment due to his connection with Julius and others that there was never an eyebrow or question raised about his bringing his son to hang out in such an environment. Going there with him was the highlight of my week; I loved being around that crew and felt welcomed in a strange way even though I was 9 or 10 years old and had no business listening to the kinds of conversations I couldn't help but overhear at times.

I was there so often that I eventually even learned to cook my own hamburgers in the kitchen—mostly for myself, but occasionally for guests that would place an order, too. I will never forget how surprised I was when I learned that cooks added butter to the buns when they were being toasted to make them taste so good...I felt as if I'd been let in on an amazing secret and was always excited to deploy that previously unknown method of culinary magic when I was able to get on The B&B's grill for myself and others.

My mom would later tell me that some of the card games Pops played on those weekends had more importance than I was aware of at the time, including games that helped pay utility and medical bills that needed covering. This information also explained why I noticed my dad took the game more seriously than those around him did. He was not an avid reader at the time, but I would see him devouring books written by David Sklansky and Doyle Brunson and eventually he came to understand the advantages a player can gain by digging as deeply into theory, and odds, and position-plays, and betting habits. He was focused, and always seemed to make the right statistical or positional decisions throughout his games even when it didn't land him a pot.

In a deck of 52 cards, there are 1,326 different combinations that a player can be dealt as the first two cards ("hole cards") they receive at the beginning of a new hand when playing Texas Hold 'Em. There is a hierarchy that assigns a ranking next to each of these 1,326 combinations based on strength of cards, with two aces, or "pocket aces" being the top of the list since Aces are the high card in the game. Hole cards like a 7-3 unsuited (one spade, one heart, for example) would rank toward the bottom of that hierarchy due to the lower likelihood they will perform as strongly compared with other card combinations as the hand progresses.

Having strong hole cards in no way guarantees victory over weaker hole cards throughout any hand being played, but waiting for stronger starting hands before you enter a hand is typically an advantage that successful players utilize more frequently than poor players who rush in to play with any hand that's dealt to them.

I learned over the course of many years that my dad tended to favor the starting hands that may not look as strong at the beginning, but when played wisely could take down the higher-confidence hole cards being thrown around by weaker players. He'd been an underdog his entire life and sometimes he liked hole cards that resembled that background.

As I got older, he taught me more and more about the nuances of poker, which led to some of the best and most frequent conversations we had. I started to see the game as he did, and I quickly noticed that my dad's view of poker didn't always end with a physical stack of cards. His immersion in the game got so deep that he would often refer to *people* or entire situations as hole cards, or the two starting cards you receive in Texas Hold 'Em, instead of regular adjectives that everyone else would use in normal conversation.

"This guy is *Pocket 10's,* man—just smooth and crafty…you never see him coming. F*cking love him." This was how he would describe the friend he had from The B&B who was over installing illegal premium cable chips for our home's televisions. And I knew exactly what he was talking about when he described him as such; he didn't have to explain a thing to me.

If he was upset about a fast-food restaurant forgetting part of his meal, he'd accuse the place of having a "Seven-Deuce off-suit crew" working that day, and when everyone else was confused by such language, I never had to ask him anything. If I really pissed him off, say if I forgot to close the garage door or misdealt a hand during a poker game, he'd call me an "Ace-Queen,"—which might sound like a relatively good pair of hole cards to most players because of its position high in the hierarchy, but I knew from years of hearing him complain about how many times those two particular hole cards had broken his heart and how much money he'd lost on them. I knew it wasn't a compliment.

Wednesday nights became his consistent night to play at what once was the Trump Casino in East Chicago and the Horseshoe Casino in Hammond, Indiana. When I first moved to Chicago after college, I used to meet him there after work occasionally on those evenings and spend all night playing in the same room but at a different table than he. Every couple hours we'd check in with each other to go grab a hot dog and talk about whatever streaks or bad beats we'd just endured, then head back to the tables separately to get back at it again.

He used to love telling me about "The Rooskies," a group of Russian doctors and lawyers he would play next to almost every week that respected his game and would always give him grief for taking their money at the table. Part of me thinks Pops liked the fact that he was playing against people with well-respected professions like doctors and lawyers because it helped justify the time and effort he spent playing there and being next to what he had to assume were tremendous members of their community. And another part of me thinks he really liked the fact that he was better than they were at something they cared about, and taking *their* money was even more enjoyable than from those that didn't attend fancy colleges and post-graduate schools.

Poker was a cool thing the two of us shared together for many years. He took me to Las Vegas when I turned 21, and we played in the Bellagio poker room for three straight days filled with numerous uninterrupted 12-hour sessions at the table. I don't recall either of us sitting down together for one breakfast, lunch, or dinner that took more than five minutes to eat, and I don't know if either of us slept on the beds we had in the hotel room we reserved, but both of us were in heaven.

I remember having a somewhat serious nasal surgery in college during the summer heading into my senior year, and everyone in my family being extremely confused as to why my dad would volunteer to take care of me in post-recovery at my house on campus. I know he loved me, but he wasn't exactly the type that would raise his hand and volunteer to drive more than three hours to take close care of me in that sort of state. When my mother pulled out of the driveway to head home after her shift was complete and Pops arrived, it became clearer as he looked me right in my swollen, bloodshot eyes and said, "Caesar's Louisville poker room is 75 minutes from here, let's go." And off we went.

Pops was a multiple-time winner of a weekly tournament that drew hundreds of the area's best players at the Trump Casino in the early 2000's, which is an incredible feat. He went on to play in a variety of World Series of Poker Tournaments in Las Vegas where literally the best players in the world gather for a month of events each year in pursuit of an almighty WSOP bracelet and the lifelong bragging rights and timeless respect that come with it. One year when he was playing in the tournament, he was captured on the ESPN television broadcast, and I must have heard from everyone I knew that they saw the famous "OD" playing at the World Series and taking on the best and kicking their tails.

My dad took me to see Julius for the final time when he was getting hospice care at his home. I was 12 years old and hadn't seen anyone I cared about in that sort of state before, so I was startled when we walked in and I think my dad could sense that by how quiet I was. Julius was normally the person I wanted to talk with the most, and now I found myself at a loss for words seeing him so compromised and near death.

Thankfully the nurse broke up the silence that was hanging over our space in the room as she approached his bed to administer care. She was young and seemed a bit overwhelmed by taking on someone as ornery as Julius, but she was very capable and was as direct as she could be when she said,

"OK Julius, time for your shot."

"Make it a Jack Daniels goddammit and don't come back till it's ready," he managed to mutter. For a 12 year old, that was about the coolest way someone could stare down their dwindling health, and I thought the words fit him perfectly. The poor woman had to have absolutely hated that job.

Julius passed shortly thereafter, and his death was tough for me to process. I remember trying to hold back tears while I was walking up to bat in a Little League baseball game the day I learned he'd died and getting a hug from the umpire when I got to the plate, because she also knew Julius from The B&B and she knew how much he meant to me. When I had my First Communion a couple years prior, Julius came to my party and wrote me a card that said, "To the Best, From the Best," which I kept near my bedstand, and I was thinking about that phrase the entire game to get through it all.

People like Julius and the other wild cast of characters I interacted with at The B&B and across Osceola growing up taught me how to handle myself around a very wide variety of people. It taught me how to get to know people from extremely different backgrounds and situations and lifestyles, and it taught me how to withhold judgment until I got to know them better on a personal level. Hearing stories about how Julius once tossed the famed Paul "Golden Boy" Hornung out of his bar for being disrespectful made me love him even more. Julius did not give a shit who you were or what type of clout you had. There was a code to be followed and if you didn't abide by it, you were out, even if you were a Heisman winner at Notre Dame who went on to win Super Bowls and MVP awards for the Green Bay Packers in the NFL.

As an outsider it would be easy to denigrate people like Julius, and I do not *celebrate* any of his misdeeds or obfuscations around the law, but he and others like him extended a type of kindness and friendship to me that had an undeniably positive impact on my life, and I loved him for it.

There are countless people like Julius I encountered growing up in Osceola whom I felt similarly about, and it was always them that would come to mind and make me feel protective when folks from other places seemed too quick to judge us and look down on the entire town as being "white trash" or people lacking whatever level of sophistication they thought their town had. That was always bullshit. I knew better. Everyone who lived there knew better. It was the outsiders' lack of knowledge about something they didn't quite understand that made them think that way, and they weren't right for doing so in my opinion. These people were my friends and they were my family and I loved them for everything they were—and weren't—and what they helped me become over the years.

Looking back, I wish my own behavior had been a better example that would have put Osceola in a more positive light growing up rather than contributing to its somewhat disreputable standing. In some ways I think I helped that effort as I got older, but in many others I know I fell short, even with what I thought were good intentions while living there as a kid, and I regret that.

Being from Osceola neither defines me nor is it part of my identity, the way I thought it was when I was growing up—but it is a part of who I am, and to the extent there are positive traits within me others find admirable today I can still trace at least a portion of them back to something I learned while growing up there, and I am beyond grateful for that.

Years after Julius died and new ownership took over, my dad got into an altercation at The B&B—which wasn't completely out of the norm— but this time he received a lifetime ban. There have been countless men who have received this "lifetime ban" at The B&B, only to show up the next morning laughing at what transpired the night before while ordering a Bloody Mary and have everything continue as if nothing had happened. But this was personal for my dad, and he never wanted to set foot in the place again, especially because there was never one picture of Julius that was hung there in memory of a man that meant so much to the establishment's history and Osceola's history. And I didn't blame him one bit.

I'm sure my dad would describe Julius as "Pocket Aces" if he were to pick hole cards that would fit the man, which is the best starting hand you can be dealt in Texas Hold 'Em —and I would agree. I loved the guy and to assign him as anything short of the best hole cards would be an affront. But Julius never really needed aces to win. He usually stacked the deck in his favor and paid off the dealer to throw favorable cards his way from the bottom when no one else was looking and challenge you to double your bets. But I think Julius himself would have preferred to be called "Pocket Tens" just like my dad, something strong and capable and dangerous, but a little less flashy—the winning hand that you just never saw coming.

CHAPTER 12

GOING FROM 0 TO 1 IS A BIGGER JUMP THAN 1 TO 6

Complete strangers seem to gain way more confidence than I've ever had at any point in my life whenever they see me and Colleen out together with our kids in public.

There is an uncanny surge of adrenaline that flows through their entire being and nuggets of wisdom they immediately acquire on seeing us, which compels them to share out loud or their body might spontaneously combust. It almost never fails.

Here's a pretty typical situation:

The Seven of Us: (eating ice cream and talking by ourselves, away from others)

Complete Stranger: (enters scene incredibly quickly with something apparently very exciting to tell us): "Looks like you've got your hands full there, huh?!"

The Seven of Us: "Yeah, we love it, these guys are the best. Have a good day."

Complete Stranger: (this time looking directly at me and Colleen only): "Y'all do know how those kids keep getting made, right? Riiight?!?!"

The Seven of Us: (nothing)

Complete Stranger: "I see you're playing that *Zone Defense*, huh?!"

The Seven of Us: (continue eating ice cream)

Complete Stranger: "Bet you're real excited about that college tuition and wedding expenses coming up, yessirreeboooy! Oh man, *tons* of money!"

The Seven of Us: (still eating ice cream)

Complete Stanger: "Yeah that's too many kids see you later."

End Scene.

We realize most people rarely mean any real harm with their comments and are just using filler to engage in a conversation, but this approach sure does strike us as odd. We know tons of families with 4, 5, 6, 9 kids, and even one with 13 kids—so what we're doing with our crew doesn't ever seem like it's all that noteworthy. But people have an opinion when they see us, and we hear about it often.

They look at the five young kids and think that it's a jump that's too far for them to take, which is a totally reasonable opinion that we respect and understand completely. We see it differently for us obviously, but we totally get why it's not for everyone. The funniest part about it, however, is that I don't even consider the piece they tend to pay most attention to the biggest part of the story.

My thought has always been that to get to that jump of having 5 kids or 3 kids or 1 kid, the biggest and most important jump was the mindset of going from 0 other people that I was living for, devoted to, committed to—that I would put above my own needs and happiness and would love more than anything and choose to live with and serve —to 1. Just 1 other person whom I would choose above myself and live with to build a life. And that jump took place long before the kids came along. That's when everything changes.

The importance of jumping from 0 to 1 cannot be overstated, because it represents the conscious and thoughtful decision you make and act on to love someone more than you love yourself. No one can be forced to do this. No one can be coerced into it. You're choosing to sacrifice the world in which you put yourself first and you decide to live for someone else, which allows you to be part of the kind of love that makes everything around you bigger. If done properly, this leap from 0 to 1 can be the single biggest jump you ever take and becomes the platform from which all other future incremental leaps will be made, because you now know that you're capable of doing so.

I have a grandmother who gave birth to 11 children, and when I used to ask how she had time to love every kid equally, she would always say the same thing:

"Love doesn't divide; it only multiplies. The more love you give, the bigger you get and the more capacity you gain to give even more to those you love."

I like to think of that when I picture her going from 0 to 1 in marrying my grandfather, then both wildly expanding on that together with more and more leaps taken over the years.

This idea of jumping from 0 to 1 isn't exclusive to getting married or having kids or being in a relationship with someone. There are many people in the world who have jumped to 1 by devoting themselves to an ideal that's bigger than themselves, to a cause they find worthy, to a religion—all having little to do with intimate relationships or marriages in the traditional sense. That jump does the same thing in their lives and represents the vision of serving others.

And just because a particular jump to 1 doesn't last forever—divorces happen, relationships can fall apart, visions can change and cause the ideals you're pursuing to differ—it's the fact that you've proven you were capable of jumping to 1 in the first place that matters. That is what will set you up for future leaps when you pick yourself back up and feel ready to do so.

My experience jumping to 1 had to do with getting married and what I learned was simple: deciding if you want to be married and deciding whom to marry is one of the most important decisions you can make in your life, because it will impact nearly every facet of what you engage in as an individual throughout the remainder of your time and will in many ways determine the level of fulfillment and ability to perform in those activities. Making sure that your partner shares similar values, that you share a vision for the kind of goals and life you want to have together, that they can challenge you and help you become the best version of yourself, and that they're as committed and devoted to you and are willing to give 100 percent of themselves and be committed to your partnership, even when it isn't easy.

Raising two kids typically involves more activity and time and effort than raising one kid, and three kids is typically busier than two kids, and four kids is typically busier than three, etc. We know this to be true, because we've experienced it while both of us were also working full-time jobs trying to grow in our careers and trying to be contributing members to the community around us and trying to be good to the friends and families we're part of. It's all very busy; we get it.

We also learned that all of the time and stress and sacrifice and effort associated with raising our children and living our very busy lives together is far more manageable and enjoyable when we are both aligned to the expectations of what we're pursuing and are fully devoted to each other while going through all of it together because that's what we both *want*. The sacrifice is justified by the meaning and fulfillment the effort brings, even on bad days.

There are hours and days and sometimes entire months that are way more stressful and frustrating and challenging to deal with than others, when you're not exactly seeing rainbows and butterflies with your partner or your children or society at large. It helps to have someone you love and trust to get you through those difficult times, and you're going to need that consistent person in your corner. I don't see any path in life that I would consider "easy" or one where you're able to avoid challenges, especially if you are trying your best to be in a committed relationship and raising a family—opening yourself up to the kind of love with which you're capable of getting to 1 can be all you need get through it all, and in a way that provides more fulfillment.

There is nothing noble in and of itself in getting married or having kids. There are countless parents and spouses that are awful to each other, making the experience far worse and miserable for everyone involved. I don't see much good in that and, worse yet, their unwillingness to live up to the responsibility of taking on those important roles can act as a deterrent to those they're negatively impacting around them, which could derail them from wanting to be associated with these positive acts in the future.

I believe the nobility of these endeavors is in the aim and how you go about putting *action* behind the intent that you're aiming at throughout your time spent in these types of roles. The spirit you bring while performing. The willingness to pick up large amounts of responsibility and doing so in a strong and capable fashion. It is in the sacrifice. It is in the joy you're bringing to those you love and the sacrifices you make to improve their lives, to provide them with the kind of security and warmth and companionship and love they cherish and deserve.

Like any man dedicated to being a husband and father and professional and adult with responsibilities, I have missed my share of golf outings, poker nights, guys' trips, etc., due to the responsibilities I have and my desire to perform well for those in my care. There is no martyrdom in missing these things. I want to be where I am and am not resentful when I see others out enjoying time away. I also make sure I take plenty of time for myself and get away to do those activities I love whenever I can, because the responsibilities I am choosing are not a jail and are not intended to "hold me down" in any way at all.

If someone asked me for the best professional career advice I could provide, I would say: Marry the right person.

If someone asked me for the best health advice I could provide, I would say: Marry the right person.

If someone asked me for the best financial advice I could provide, I would say: Marry the right person.

Find a worthy cause or partner or ideal you're passionate about and when the time is right, make the jump from 0 to 1. I have found that my life got exponentially bigger when I had the courage and vulnerability to do so.

Plus, I've come to find that compared with the joy of having five kids, free time and disposable income are overrated, anyways.

CHAPTER 13

HOW NOT TO GO TO COLLEGE

The experience I had leading up to attending college was not something I would recommend to anyone who is interested in pursuing higher education of any kind in a meaningful way.

At no point during my high school years did I think past the grade I was in at the time. At no point did I develop a plan on what post-graduation life would look like for me. And at no point did I seriously apply myself to explore what skills and interests I had that could be expanded on in a setting like a university or a trade school or the Military offer to young people striving toward personal growth.

Not exactly what I would consider "vision work."

For most of high school, I had no intention of going to college and was fine with the idea that I would stick around Osceola, Indiana, and "just sort of figure it out" somehow, even though I had no marketable skills or talents that I could offer the few places of employment that were available where I grew up. Yet it all sounded very solid to me. Rooted. Structured. *Strategic.* In my head and in conversations, I remember having, like, *real confidence* when I would talk about this "plan" and would always be confused when I would see the expression on other people's faces as if I'd simultaneously grown three noses when the topic came up.

But all of that changed with one brazen lie I told to a girl I wanted to impress, and a hopeless attempt to mimic an older classmate that I barely knew at all.

On the first day of my senior year of high school, I walked into a conversation with a group of people I hadn't seen much over the summer and was excited to reconnect with. I puttered around their semi-circle trying to sneak into the discussion, but quickly became more than a little self-conscious and regretted putting myself there when I heard the topic of college being reviewed. At that moment I wanted nothing more than to find my closer friends who were probably arguing about whether they thought a Bear or a Shark would win in a fight, or how many marshmallows they thought they could fit in their mouths at once. *Those are my people*, I thought. Instead, I was listening to these very smart classmates complaining about having had to take both the ACT and the SAT prep courses over the summer.

I came home from a vacation just a few weeks prior to this conversation and, due to flight delays, we hadn't landed at the airport until around 1 a.m. I'd almost forgotten that I'd signed up for SATs that started at 7 a.m. that day and stumbled to the table with an unsharpened pencil and slight limp from a hang-gliding slipup I had picked up while away. I hadn't taken any prep classes, I hadn't read any books related to the test, and I didn't have any clue about what was coming— but I managed to get through it and scored a mediocre 1020. I didn't know what a score of 1020 even meant, but after I received the score, the SAT was just another thing I thought I'd never have to think about again as I headed toward the completion of high school.

One of the girls in the group I was talking with was in the middle of explaining that she'd received early acceptance at Brown or Cornell or some other school that didn't include a state's name in it that I'd never heard of before, and then, without even putting a period on the end of her sentence—she immediately shifted the conversation over to me for no reason at all and blurted out:

"And what about you, David? Have you been accepted or decided where you're going yet?"

I looked behind me before answering to make sure she wasn't talking to someone else—but to my surprise when I turned around, no one was there—so I took a quick swallow to add a little saliva to a mouth that was now the driest it had ever been in my life and said the first thing that came to my mind. I didn't even consider correcting her and letting her know my name was actually Dennis.

"Indiana. Really excited. It's an awesome school. Can't wait."

"Oh, cool. Yeah, my cousin went there and loved it. Congratulations."

I am pretty sure the group continued talking, but I couldn't hear anything because my ears were ringing like the Bells of St. Mary's and my head temporarily left my shoulders as soon as I got through my lie hoping it would go through.

Indiana? Indiana State? Indiana Tech? Indiana School for Boys Who Tell Bad Fibs? I wasn't 100 percent sure yet, but that's what I said.

One thing I was sure about in that moment was that when I was in 8th grade, there was a senior named Ricky Siri that I idolized. He was a star football and basketball player at the high school I would attend, and to top it off he seemed like one of the nicest guys in the entire world. I was friends with his sister who was my age and I thought he was the greatest thing ever because he was so talented at the two sports I was struggling so much to be good at.

He would always say hello to me whenever I saw him, and he never made me feel like the annoying younger hanger-on trying to get his attention. When I was put on the spot and asked where I was going to college, for some reason I recalled his sister telling me that Ricky had attended Indiana University after high school and immediately thought to myself, "Well, sh*t, if Indiana is good enough for Ricky Siri, then it's good enough for me."

And that was that. So, I said Indiana.

After lying right to that nice girl's face and to all her friends, I walked into the guidance counselor's offices and filled out an application to Indiana University on the spot. I sent the application in, went on with the start of senior year, sort of forgot about doing it altogether, then on my birthday in October a couple months later I received an acceptance letter in the mail. I hadn't taken an official college visit anywhere (including to Indiana) and didn't apply to any other school. But off I was to become a Hoosier.

My parents would have supported any path I chose after high school—they were always in my corner backing me up, which is a blessing I hope every child is lucky enough to experience firsthand. But they never attended college and neither did most of the friends and neighbors who hung out with my family, so I don't think they knew how to help plan or prepare for their first child to get through the process at the time. Plus, I was 17 years old and should have been capable of doing it on my own. My grades were always very good, so we never had to really check in with each other about how school was going or have tough talks around projects that were due—I just got the work done on my own and kept that world to myself without needing their input or attention.

My time at the beginning of college was littered with examples of me not quite understanding my surroundings, not understanding what opportunities existed that I could take advantage of, and not grasping what was taking place around me in general. What was happening for me—walking aimlessly around a huge, beautiful campus where it appeared young people gathered primarily to have fun and party—was clearly different for others who were more goal-oriented and further emotionally developed and mature than I was at the time.

I didn't know how to select a major that I was interested in; I was still not thinking past any year, or month, or day I was living in at the time; and I didn't even bother to purchase books for most of the classes that I signed up for. I would get lost around campus most days and pop into large lecture hall classes that I wasn't even registered for just to listen in on what other people were learning about, without bothering to study for exams I had in my own classes. I was way more concerned with trying to establish myself with friends and projecting an image of something that I knew wasn't ideal for the long-term, but I wasn't quite sure how to prepare for a career at the time and acted as if it didn't matter, either.

I have a hard time believing that any time or experience is truly "wasted." There is almost always something gained or learned even when we don't quite see it at the time. But academically speaking, and in terms of setting myself up for future professional success, it's hard not to consider my first two years wasted compared with what could have taken place in college with more planning, focus, discipline, vision, and effort to expand myself rather than holding on to who I was before.

I felt as if I was betraying the friends and associates in my hometown if I didn't do the late-night scene and "represent." There just could not have been a dumber way to think and act, especially when you've been given such a great opportunity like going to college. I felt protective of the lifestyle my older friends were living back home and tried to bring all of it with me into an environment that just didn't quite support it. When I would visit home, I'd get self-conscious when I would get called "College Boy" from people that automatically thought I was looking down on them when I would answer that I was attending IU. I would quickly shift my behaviors to reflect the world from home rather than the world I was part of at school. I felt caught between two environments and didn't know how to handle either one properly.

At one point during my sophomore year, I borrowed a friend's car to drive to Chicago and missed two days of classes to try out for "Slamball." Yes, Slamball: the short-lived professional start-up full-contact basketball league that placed humongous trampolines throughout the court and promoted massive collisions with high-flying dunks. Before leaving for the Slamball tryouts I think I told my roommate he could keep my books and clothes that I was leaving behind, because he'd never see me again since I was on my way to becoming an international athletic superstar. I thought that Slamball was going to be more beneficial for me than graduating college.

Slamball. Think about that for a second in terms of where I was at in the college process and where my level of maturity was.

After arriving at the sacred "Hoops Gym" where the tryouts were held and getting cut almost immediately, I took what had to be the longest drive of all time back to Bloomington and explained to my roommate that I was going to need those clothes and books back after all.

Instead of returning to Osceola, I decided to stay on campus in Bloomington to take summer classes after my sophomore year, which gave me the opportunity to learn and listen more without falling into the trap of being a social superstar. I had so much more time to myself and was able to start really thinking why I was there, how I could make more of the opportunity I had in front of me, and how to expand myself to become more than I had been in the past. I started reading novels for the first time. I started really appreciating nature and would walk around campus for hours by myself. I started working out more frequently and began dedicating way more time and devotion to the rugby team I'd been part of and found ways to take on leadership roles on and off the field to improve the club. All of this helped me see that positive results came around when I took myself seriously and treated myself as someone who had a future that mattered rather than the type of guy who was only looking for a fun time.

I started really paying attention to the successful people around me and noticed ways they operated that I respected. I started to pick up on the type of vocabulary they used when they spoke, what topics they were interested in, how they were humble in front of others, how they took on larger amounts of responsibilty than I was, and how they seemed a bit more comfortable in their skin than I was. An awakening started that really made me think about what I would need to do to get closer to the person I knew I wanted to become. I didn't feel the need to copy anyone; I just started seeing consistent trends that seemed to gravitate toward strength and respect that I thought would be a better alternative for me to pursue.

I would notice my roommates' stories about their families and upbringings and take mental notes on which parts sounded ideal and began making lists for the first time about what I could do to put myself in a position to have something similar in the future. I would watch their parents come into town for dinner at a restaurant and would listen so intently to the types of conversations they would have. I'd notice the way they would dress, the way they conducted themselves in public, and the way they would describe their professions and responsibilities. Everything began to fascinate me.

This does not mean I was comparing my family or my experiences growing up in a *negative* way—I wasn't. I just started noticing so many *differences* for the first time, good and bad, and started to finally grasp the concept that I could develop any kind of life for myself that I wanted in the future, even if I had no clue how to get there yet. Looking back, that was a good start compared with the drifting I'd done before.

There were not any real step-changes in my academic performance that I would consider impressive as my junior/senior years came around, but some of my habits did improve. I began to get a better grasp on how to learn from professors and guest lecturers who were obviously incredibly capable in their fields of expertise. I started volunteering occasionally with the IU Student Foundation and spent a little time helping at a place called "The Rise," which helped survivors of domestic violence and their children find their way back safely into society. My few weeks there were mostly spent teaching the kids how to play basketball and running around the fields to give their parents a much-needed break during the afternoons, but I loved it and I could tell the children enjoyed it too. That felt great to me.

I started attending mass regularly by myself on Sunday evenings at St. Paul on campus, and for the first time felt a true connection to the Catholic Church after growing up attending church events and mass not terribly often or consistently. By the time I finished my degree, I felt that I was finally on way my toward transforming into someone I was way prouder of than when I began. I was more confident about liking the things I liked and being myself rather than a projection of who I wanted people to think I was.

The Liberal Arts have become an easy target for criticism recently, but I cannot overstate how valuable that path of education was for me. I had the chance to finally learn my own language, to study topics and ideas that I would think about for the rest of my life. Even if they weren't directly associated with a career I had in mind, they gave me the confidence and the ability to learn in a manner that I appreciated then and appreciate even more so now.

The last time I saw or spoke to Ricky Siri was something like, maybe, 1997? The conversation probably went like this:

Me: Hey Ricky! What's up? How are you?!
Ricky: Oh, hey man.
Ricky: (walks away)
Me: That was so awesome. I love that guy.

But, serendipitously enough, that dude ended up being one of the reasons I decided to go to college and was the main reason I applied to Indiana, which was something that changed the trajectory of my life in a significant way after all was said and done.

Did I have fun? Unequivocally. To this day I *love* Indiana University. I made many meaningful memories and created great friendships with amazing people and had experiences that made me better than what I was, which are things that I will carry with me for a lifetime.

But could I have done better? Could I have worked to develop more lasting relationships? Could I have committed myself to begin thinking about "where the puck was heading" in my life vs. "where the puck was" and take better advantage of the opportunities, people, and resources around me while I was there? Without a doubt. Especially during my freshman and sophomore years.

I am hopeful that my children will be much better prepared for their college experience and make more of it than I did, especially in the beginning. They will make their own stupid youthful mistakes and will lack direction in their own way, undoubtedly. But when they get started, I want them to be more self-assured and confident than I was, and self-aware enough to pursue the studies and activities that will spur their growth into the person they want to become. I am hopeful the environment they're part of growing up in gives them a view of opportunities they can take advantage of, and I hope they strike a better balance of having the kind of fun I enjoyed while still putting in the necessary work to set them up for future success.

And if they don't? Then who knows? It will be their life by that time and my goal will be to help them wherever I can to make the most of themselves.

Even if that means driving them to a Slamball tryout when the league makes its triumphant comeback in the year 2035.

CHAPTER 14

GEORGIA ON OUR MIND

In 2019, Colleen and I had a big decision to make. After meeting with one my company's executives during a trip to Santa Monica, California, in July of that year, I was given the opportunity to move to Atlanta so I could work out of the Georgia-Pacific corporate headquarters and eventually take on the kind of expanded roles that I thought would put me on the career path I'd always wanted. I loved the company I was working for, and I knew this would be a truly great development for me professionally, but it was incredibly challenging for us to decide whether we should leave the family, community, friends, and wonderful life that we'd built for ourselves over the past six years in Wheaton, Illinois. We had five young kids present and futures to think about and picking up and moving across the country would not be a painless process for any of us.

Colleen moved a few times for her dad's career while growing up and often talked about such positive memories of the different experiences her family enjoyed together while doing so. We knew we were always up for a fun family adventure, having already moved to and from Greenville, South Carolina, earlier in our marriage and could not have had a better time throughout that journey, and after months of discussions and scenario projecting, we made a leap of faith and decided that going to Atlanta was the right move to make for us.

We told the kids on October 3rd, 2019, and let our friends and family know shortly thereafter. From that day, the two months leading up to the move in mid-December were nothing short of a living, breathing fever dream. Getting our house staged, decorated, and prepared to sell; interviewing and selecting a real estate agent; listing the house on the market; keeping the house clean and showing the house to all of the potential buyers; getting paperwork from schools and doctors and dentists and municipalities arranged that could be transferred to what would be our new contacts in Georgia; flying to Atlanta multiple times to find new schools and tour houses to determine where we would live; selling a house that we'd loved; buying a new house in a brand new city without fully understanding which location would be best to buy in; packing up all of the possessions in our Wheaton house; arranging for temporary housing in Atlanta where we'd live while our home was getting updated; closing out all active local memberships and groups we were part of in Chicago; canceling utilities; setting up new utilities; alerting our banks and credit card companies of the upcoming move; arranging final playdates with the kids' friends they likely wouldn't see again, and doing the same with our adult friends; and finally moving two parents, five kids, and one au pair across the country, all while the both of us were still working full-time jobs and getting our kids through all of their school homework, sports practices and games, Halloween, Thanksgiving, and Christmas activities that lead up to December 15th.

I'd lost a little over 15 pounds from the stress associated with taking care of everything that needed to get accomplished throughout the process, and Colleen was just as physically and emotionally fried as I was by the time moving day came along.

Our friends organized a going-away party for our family the day before our move at a bar in downtown Wheaton called "Dry City" and more than 200 people came through to wish us well and say goodbye. I found myself feeling far more emotional than I expected throughout the time leading up to us leaving and did my best to publicly and sincerely acknowledge how grateful we were to be part of such a special group of people's lives. The next day, we were off. I drove by myself in the most tightly packed minivan ever seen in human history 13 hours straight from Chicago to Atlanta the morning of December 15th and had the rest of the family flying in that evening, so my job was to get to the rental house and unpack the clothes and possessions we'd need and be at Hartsfield-Jackson Atlanta Airport in time to pick them up and get them home for our first night as a family together as residents of Georgia.

Part of the relocation package provided to us included two months of temporary housing, so rather than moving into the house we purchased that was in dire need of restoration from top to bottom, we found a fully furnished, unique log cabin rental that was only a couple miles away from the home we would eventually move into.

I was talking with the landlord when I learned that this log cabin was the oldest residential home in all of Atlanta…it was originally built in the early 1800's in Tennessee, and over a period had been transferred to Georgia piece by piece in its entirety where it now stood fully constructed once again. I thought it would be *beyond* cool to have our kids live in the oldest house in Atlanta and give them an awesome historical experience and I couldn't wait to share the news with them.

It turns out, the only downside to living in the oldest house in Atlanta, is that you live in the Oldest. House. In. Atlanta. It was apparent right away as I unloaded the car that night that parts of the home were in their original form and that the flooring was prone to giving massive splinters to those walking around in anything less than steel-toed shoes. But I still thought it would be great.

When the family entered the log cabin for the first time together that evening, 6 out of 7 of us were hopeful, excited, and feeling exhilarated as we were starting our newest chapter together in a beautiful and vibrant new city. Our 2-year-old son Daniel, however, put forth a projectile vomit stronger and more furious than anything we'd seen from him before as soon as he set his first foot inside the log cabin, and wasn't exactly feeling the same cheery vibes the rest of us were. We didn't know it at the time, but looking back, Danny throwing up after walking into the log cabin was a literary device commonly deployed in the writing world known as "foreshadowing" in terms of what was about to hit the entire world just two short months later.

The couple months we spent in the log cabin didn't quite put an end to the fever dream we'd just endured while leaving Wheaton, but we were getting through it. We had a fun family Christmas together and got to do so outside in the warm sunshine because we were now living in Atlanta. We started the kids at their new schools, I was taking the MARTA train downtown to the office every morning, and we did our best to meet as many people as we could to accelerate our acclimation process. We were embracing the change and making the best of everything we could control.

When she wasn't working or taking care of the family, all of Colleen's time was spent acting as a general contractor as she led a remodeling effort that rivals anything that's ever been captured on Chip and Joanna Gaines's reality TV series. She developed the entire vision and plan for the renovation and created a masterpiece. She's always been good at decorating, with a great eye for knowing what type of designs work well for the homes we've lived in, but what she did to this particular home was above and beyond - especially considering that she was doing so in such a short amount of time, with a carpenter and team that she'd never met before, and on a budget that was likely a fifth the size it should have been for the scope of the project. Walls were removed, new spaces were created, appliances and floors were totally redone. She transformed a house that hadn't been touched on the inside for 30 years into a gorgeous, modern, comfortable, spacious home for our family, and she did it all while carrying a huge amount of additional weight and responsibility with work and family demands never being higher.

We moved into our home in mid-February 2020 and were starting to really feel settled. The kids finally had their rooms and closets to store their clothes and we could finally start living a normal life with the kind of day-to-day consistency we'd been yearning for since announcing our move the previous October. When we didn't have school, practice, and games to attend, we spent most of our time walking around "The Branches" neighborhood, which felt more like a national forest compared with the suburbs we were used to in Chicago. There were beautiful, massive, lush Georgia pine trees everywhere we looked, with a vast array of wild plants and grasses every shade of green that stretched in all directions. It was invigorating to live in an area that was brimming with wildlife. We'd see deer on our front lawn most mornings, and would often see coyotes, owls, and hawks. We also saw more snakes than we cared for, but that too was something we sort of loved because it was so rare where we were from. Plus, we had two incredible families, the Yorks and Cochrans, that lived next door to us on each side that had young children that matched up to ours so well that we became fast friends, which made us feel right at home.

News surrounding COVID had been growing more prevalent since December 2019, but it was primarily impacting foreign countries and didn't seem to have a direct tie to what was happening in the United States. In February 2020, I was receiving strange requests related to supply planning concerns and dependability of exports from the customers I was working with, but there still wasn't a sweeping concern on a domestic front that caused people to worry too much.

We'd kept in contact with most of our close friends since moving away from Wheaton and were excited that a few of them made plans to come visit us on spring break to see our new city and spend quality time together. We were continuing our integration into Atlanta and couldn't wait to show our friends the new life we were on our way to building.

But on March 11, 2020, it all stopped. Literally. Everything.

Everyone has that one indelible moment when they realized that COVID was going to change the fabric of their lives forever, and ours happened while watching a basketball game on television. We've been huge NBA fans for years, and when the league made the unprecedented decision to announce the cancelation of its season that fateful night, it sent an undeniable and immediate signal across the world that nothing would be the same from that moment on. Seemingly every domino across the planet began to fall for everyone everywhere, and the impact on our transition into a new city was as thick and real as the pollen in the air.

The sports leagues we'd just joined in Atlanta were canceled. The swim/tennis neighborhood club we had been so excited to join was shut down. The schools that we'd just joined were shut down. We couldn't congregate with any of the few neighbors we had just met. The reason we moved our family to Atlanta was to integrate myself more closely with work at the office, and that was now completely gone, and nobody had a clue when it would return.

Like all students across the U.S., our kids began to Zoom their way through school—but their online lessons were with classmates who essentially amounted to complete strangers whom they'd met only a couple weeks before and hadn't had a chance to become friends with yet, which made that process even more bizarre for them. Days and weeks came and went in a blurry haze in March and April 2020, with no one certain about what frightening new developments would pop up around the next corner and an eerie feeling of fear and confusion was present in the eyes of most people you encountered.

Workers across the U.S. began remotely navigating their way through their jobs, which I was more accustomed to after years of working in sales, but this was obviously different and represented a sea change for *everyone*, since it was now nearly 100 percent of corporate employees who were at home trying to balance work with every other responsibility they had without being able to roam freely through society, for the first times in their lives.

Our family made the most of the situation given the awful circumstances, and we were lucky compared with others, even though we had five very young kids to manage through what sometimes felt like an unmanageable situation. We were pool owners for the first time, and since we lived in Atlanta that meant that we could swim outside in the middle of March, which was about as foreign a concept as we Midwesterners could imagine. Our home had a huge court that I'd transformed into a full-length basketball area that we played on for hours at a time. We spent most of our time together outside and playing fun games together to keep everyone's mind off the ever-expanding pandemic that was raging across the world.

It was usually at night after the kids were in bed that Colleen and I would catch up on how each of us was doing and check in to see where we were physically and emotionally in that moment. We talked often about how grateful we were that we both still had jobs, that our family was healthy, that we had such a fun a home to share as a family, and that our kids had their own built-in community of siblings to play with, since they couldn't see anyone else at that time. But beyond that gratitude were a few more difficult feelings and questions to process that only seemed to grow stronger as COVID continued to alter how the world was operating.

When would we see our aging parents and siblings again? When and how would we able to become part of this new community if no one knew who we were, and we could not congregate with anyone? We used to joke to ourselves, "No one invites a family of seven over for dinner on a *good day*, let alone *during a pandemic!*" Did we want to keep living in a place where we could be strangers for the next few years, and what would that do to our kids' overall development? It was among the strangest times in history to have moved a family of seven across the country, and we were starting to wonder what our options looked like in this new environment.

So, in May of 2020, I had a conversation with my company to ask what would happen if we decided that Wheaton was now the best possible place for my family to reside, given how much the world had changed since we'd arrived in Georgia six months before. This was not an easy discussion for me to initiate, in part because of how much they'd invested in getting my family to Georgia but also because I know they were aware of just how excited I was to be there for this new opportunity. I was nervous that they'd make negative judgments about my character if I broached this subject and would just as soon fire me instead of allowing me to move back to Wheaton. After talking together with Colleen for weeks on end, however, we knew that the situation we found ourselves in caused exclusively by COVID was not one that was foreseen by anyone, and that this conversation was a necessary one to have for the sake of our family, regardless of how it would land when talking through it with my employer.

Could I perform the same work from Wheaton I was now doing exclusively out of my home in Georgia? Would it be work that is fulfilling to me and valuable to the company? Could I make significant contributions to my team and to the business and continue advancing my career to gain higher levels of responsibility and compensation in the future?

When I was able to answer "yes" to those questions and others that we discussed together, my company said something along the lines of, "Sure, we get it. It's somewhat soon, but what you're saying also makes sense given how this pandemic has changed everything." And with that support, we had the blessing to go forward with what was the single most unthinkable thing that would have ever been considered in December 2019 before anyone in America knew what COVID was, and that was to begin the process of moving back to the amazing family, friends, community, and life that we had established and waiting for us in Wheaton. I cannot give my company enough credit for understanding our situation and being agreeable to what I was requesting under such unique circumstances. I told them how much it meant to us at the time, but it was hard to convey just how significant this decision was.

Watching the faces of our children when we told them the news that we were moving back to Wheaton was one of the most memorable expressions of joy, relief, and love that I can recall them feeling collectively. And once we executed another round of fever dream action items to make it all come together, we were home—this time for good. Our kids didn't care that we were leaving a beautiful pool and huge court in the backyard and one of the nicest houses we'd ever own—we just wanted to go *home*, to feel at home, and to surround ourselves around the people that mean the most to us.

After all was said and done, we spent eight months in Atlanta. We sure did quite a bit while there, even with COVID spreading across the planet and restrictions in place throughout the city…we caught an Atlanta Hawks basketball game at State Farm Center; we climbed Stone Mountain twice and Kennesaw Mountain once; we visited the Georgia Aquarium; we stayed at Callaway Gardens and swam in Robin Lake and caught fish in Mountain Creek Lake; we toured the University of Georgia campus and walked through the legendary Sanford Stadium where the football team plays; we hung out around The Battery and the new home of the Atlanta Braves; we hiked countless trails; we went to Piedmont Park and explored dozens of other parks around the area; the kids played in baseball, softball, soccer, and basketball leagues; we celebrated Evey's first reconciliation; we were in the St. Jude Girl Scouts; we took a family MARTA ride; and we seemingly walked 6,000 miles together in our neighborhood to pass the time.

We'll miss the earlier spring seasons and consistently sunny weather that Atlanta provides compared with Chicago, and it may be especially painful on those mornings when clearing 3 inches of ice off our windshield at 6 a.m. so we can drive our kids to school in -8 degree weather, but we'll still take it.

The timeframe of living in Wheaton from July 2020 through July 2021 may have been the happiest year of our family's life. That's a year that included all of us contracting COVID, all of us still enduring tons of restrictions on whom we could and couldn't see, vacations that were canceled, and weeks upon weeks of not being able to congregate closely with those we loved. But the positives we experienced during that same timeframe within our community and moments spent with family and friends are some of the most meaningful and beautiful feelings we've shared together, and I know without question what a positive impact it has had on us all.

Will I become the CEO of Georgia-Pacific while working remotely in Wheaton, Illinois? No. No I will not. But the value of what my family gained from the move back to Wheaton simply cannot be overstated, and is measured not by my current professional title but by the peace and joy in our hearts, knowing that the meaning and fulfilment we derive from living here and spending more time with those we love is worth it.

CHAPTER 15

POST UP

One of the best ways to turn a rough day around for me is to walk out to the mailbox and discover a piece of mail with my name on the center and a certified U.S. Postal Service first-class stamp affixed to the right corner of a crisp and clean rectangular envelope.

Not a whole lot beats it.

I get more excited about receiving and sending stamped mail than most people I've met, and I know that because I can see the interest completely disappear from others' faces if our conversation shifts to mail and how quickly they begin to shuffle their feet away from me as soon as I start get going into the specifics.

There is just something so indelible about receiving *real* mail from people—you remember so much more about the message when someone decides to put pen to paper, and the messages they're conveying tend to mean more to the recipient than other forms of communication. The same exact note expressed in a card instead of on a keyboard lands differently to the receiver every time, and that subtle difference in feeling that the sender is trying to convey is absolutely everything.

When I was a kid, I recall seeing my mom open a card from one of her friends and I started complaining that I didn't receive any fun mail from anyone and wished that more people had sent me letters.

"Well, Dennis—have *you* sent anyone a letter recently? Usually in order to get mail, you should start by sending some to others first," she said.

That afternoon I sent my grandparents in California a card with a drawing that I'd colored of me and some buddies playing backyard football, and a week later I received a stamped envelope back from them with a short and sweet letter written by my grandmother with a couple bucks inside. I was off to the races for the rest of my life.

When I took my first job out of college, I found myself traveling all over the country frequently and had the idea to begin sending postcards to friends and family members from all the amazing (and some not-so-amazing) cities I would visit for work. The job itself was challenging and fun for me, and I thoroughly enjoyed the opportunity to explore so many new places for the first time—but I noticed the part of the job I always looked forward to most was the flight returning back home when I would put my tray table down and hammer out 10–20 postcards over the course of a 2–3 hour flight as I was heading back toward beautiful downtown Chicago, chuckling to myself for whatever clever message I would try to come up with for each recipient.

Since that time, I have probably sent nearly 1,000 postcards—and most have not even technically been *from* me. One thing I loved doing on these postcards was writing out a message from a celebrity or prominent person from that city and sign their name as the sender when addressing them to my friends. When I'd visit Phoenix, I would send postcards to people from Charles Barkley. When I was in Nashville, it would be from Dolly Parton or Elvis. Was it low-grade mail fraud? Possibly. But was it awesome? Yes. Yes, it was.

At first my friends weren't totally sure how or why someone like Beyoncé decided to send them a postcard or why it was postmarked from "Carol Stream, IL" instead of Los Angeles—but eventually they figured out it was from me and would look forward to seeing which artist, athlete, musician, or actor was going to send them a note next.

Not every recipient would acknowledge the postcards and very few would send letters back to me in response, even to the cards that actually were signed by me—but I thought that was fine. I loved the process of creating and sending something and I loved the idea that whoever received that stamp in the mail likely had their day improved upon doing so.

For my 30th birthday, Colleen hatched up a plan that would ensure I received more responses and more stamps than I could have dreamed of—and to this day it remains one of my favorite gifts that I can remember.

I am a creature of unbreakable habit in a couple specific ways, one of which involving getting the mail. We were living in Greenville, South Carolina, the year I was turning 30. Every single day I would arrive home from my 35-minute work commute right at 6 p.m. Upon pulling into the driveway I would turn the car off, unbuckle my seatbelt, open the door to leave the car, and walk directly over to the mailbox to see if any fun mail had arrived that day. This was as consistent of an activity as brushing my teeth in the morning and giving my newborn daughter a kiss goodbye as I left the house each day.

We had a big birthday party planned the weekend I was turning 30; we'd rented a bus and reserved a suite at the Greenville Road Warriors hockey game with all the friends and neighbors we'd met since moving to South Carolina in 2011. Colleen knew that turning 30 was a milestone birthday, and even though we were excited to celebrate with so many new people we were close with, she also knew it wouldn't be quite the same as celebrating with those friends and family members we'd been close with for many years back in Chicago.

So to make up for it, starting in August of 2012, she reached out to nearly everyone I knew back home and asked that they send me a hand-made card, or note, or letter—any type of birthday wish they wanted to create would be good—as long as it came in a stamped envelope. She made the request to hundreds of people and asked that they send their completed pieces of mail to one of our neighbors' homes ahead of my birthday in October, where they would be compiled and hidden away from me until the big day.

Fast forward to the Friday afternoon of my birthday weekend, and into the cul-de-sac I come right at 6 p.m., as usual. Turn off car, unbuckle seatbelt, open door, walk to mailbox. So far, so good.

When I opened the mailbox this time, however, I was not prepared for what I saw. I noticed the door to the mailbox felt different than normal, and that it was slightly ajar without me grabbing it, but I wasn't sure why. Even when I opened the door and saw the mailbox completely stuffed with mail, I didn't allow myself to get excited because I didn't even know what I was looking at.

The box was so full, my first thought upon analyzing the scene was actually, "Oh my gosh, our mailman must have had a complete meltdown and decided to quit his job on the spot as he got to our stop—apparently shoving all the mail that was in the backseat of his car into my mailbox before speeding away in despair and anger off into the sunset. Poor guy."

It was only after pulling out each piece of mail and seeing my name on every card (albeit with my neighbor's address listed instead of mine) that I realized what was going on. I grabbed the cards out of the mailbox and stood at the end of my driveway thumbing through the cover of each one trying to wrap my head around the glory of what was in front of me. This was everything I'd ever wanted…more stamps arrived in one day than all that I had received in the past ten years combined. It was nirvana.

I staggered toward the house carefully holding onto my coveted pieces of mail when I heard a familiar voice from the open upstairs window say aloud to me while laughing, "Stamp Heaven?"

Colleen was videotaping the entire thing. She knew I would get home at that exact time. She knew I would pull into the driveway and walk directly to the mailbox. And she knew that I would have a heart attack when I finally realized what was going on. And that's exactly how it all went down.

I posted the video she captured to our family's private YouTube channel and still watch it every year on my birthday to remember how special that moment was, and every time I see it, I can recall how much it meant to me that she would organize such a thoughtful and worthwhile gift for me to enjoy. I was so blown away by the messages I received from people that it took me almost a week to read everything—after each card I would open, I would spend 15 minutes talking with Colleen about why that person was special to me, what memories I had with them from the past, and explain what the words they crafted meant to me.

We have moved five times since that birthday—and I still have the box that contains each and every letter people sent to me that year for my birthday. I can't tell you how many items Colleen and I have had to purge with each move we have gone through since 2012—but that box has made it through with us each time, and it will stay with me forever.

I know it's considered a lost art, and I know that each year fewer and fewer pieces of mail are sent from person to person with stamps. But I suggest to anyone reading this that you buck the trend and be part of something awesome. Be part of something meaningful and send letters to your friends next time you're looking to connect with them. It's fun, and they will love it.

I have an uncle who used to play "correspondence chess" with one of his friends by mail. They had a chess board that was drawn out on a sheet of paper, and they sent the board back and forth to each other via mail after every move. That might be the coolest thing I have ever heard of in my life.

Not every piece of mail you send has to be as drawn out as that example and it doesn't have to be a novel or substantial in content for the mail to be a meaningful point of connection or fun or supportive or uplifting. Just craft a note, get an envelope, stamp it, send it, and be witness to the undeniable goodness you can spread that only costs a few minutes of your time and 55 cents…or 36 cents if you choose to opt for a postcard stamp.

CHAPTER 16

ONCE UPON A TIME IN DOOR COUNTY

Shortly after Colleen and I began dating, she invited me to accompany her on a family getaway to Door County, Wisconsin, located 4 1/2 hours due north from where we were living in the city at the time. I had never heard of Door County and had no idea what to expect once we arrived, but I was excited to spend more time with Colleen and get to know her parents and siblings better, since we were both starting to see potential of a great future together as a couple.

On the drive through Wisconsin, Colleen gave me a rundown of the small towns and communities that make up the peninsula broadly referred to as "Door County" and explained a few of the attractions that had that made them special. For those coming in from Chicago as we were, the first town in Door County you encounter on Highway 42 is Sturgeon Bay, followed by Egg Harbor, Fish Creek, Ephraim, Sister Bay, then Washington Island, and Baileys Harbor on a separate highway. Each has its own downtown center with distinctive shops, restaurants, art galleries, and local services that are unique from one another, but they all share a collective culture and spirit that permeates throughout the area that connects the entire county together like patchwork.

We were staying in the town of Egg Harbor and settled into life in the North Woods with the family by sitting around the kitchen table playing cards, running through a few board games, and drinking as many Spotted Cow Ales from New Glarus Brewing Company as we could to get our trip started together. I noticed that I couldn't receive text messages, make phone calls, or send emails from my phone or laptop anywhere near the condo we stayed in due to the lack of reception, and at first I was having a tough time relaxing, thinking that I was missing something important at work that needed tending to even though I was on vacation.

We spent a good portion of our time together walking to downtown Egg Harbor and hanging out at different restaurants to a grab coffee, have a drink outside in the sunshine, enjoy a nice meal together, and survey the flurry of activity taking place as vendors and town folk prepared for the Pumpkin Patch Festival that was being held at Harbor View Park that weekend. Pumpkin Patch is an annual celebration held each fall that features live music, carnival rides, face painting, and craft-making stations, and as much draft beer, grilled bratwurst, and buttered sweet corn as you can handle. It is a perfect event in every way and is the epitome of a good time had in the Wisconsin outdoors.

The topic of favorite movies came up when we were talking together earlier at the condo and when it was my turn to chime in, I confidently stated, "Well that's easy. It's *Once Upon a Time in the West*, featuring Charles Bronson—the greatest western actor to ever live." The room fell silent and I'm sure they started to mentally question Colleen a bit on her recent dating choices. I wasn't sure her siblings knew who Charles Bronson was or had a clue as to what movie I was talking about, but it was a highly entertaining conversation and I was adamant about how great this guy was despite no one ever having heard of him.

Fast forward a few hours to our celebrating together at Pumpkin Patch and Colleen's dad proceeding to find an oil painting being sold at one of the art stands at the festival featuring a portrait of none other than the man himself, "Il Brutto," Charles Bronson. It was an Egg Harbor Miracle. He went on to purchase the Charles Bronson oil painting from the delighted artist who couldn't have possibly imagined she would sell that painting that day and surprised me with it as a gift in front of the entire family just as the sun was setting on a beautiful Saturday afternoon in Door County.

That moment sealed the first trip I took to Door County, and I couldn't have been more grateful to have found such an unexpectedly relaxing and fun destination. When I used to think of vacations, I primarily envisioned fast-action activities like arcade rooms, trampoline parks, roller coasters, and laser tag centers. Sometimes there would be a trapeze or two somewhere in there, as well as some sort of Ponderosa-style buffet with tons of ice cream and sushi and sweet potato pie that would take hours to scarf down. Not that any of that has ever happened on any vacation I ever took, but it was part of my vision every time.

After that trip, when I thought of vacations, I started to think of Door County. I started thinking of long walks and quiet time with family members, relaxing in a comfortable chair overlooking the water, finding outdoor adventures wherever they might be, and feeling exhausted at the end of a long and fun day with loved ones.

Toward the end of that first trip it all started to click: it was a *good* thing that my phone, email, and texts didn't work—it felt great to disconnect completely for a few days and recharge in ways I didn't know were necessary. It was a *good* thing that there were no national chain restaurants to eat at that I'd been to a hundred times before, or car traffic to deal with, or even stop lights that could be found anywhere throughout the county.

Since that first trip, Colleen and I (along with our kids) have gone back to Door County somewhere around 25 different times over the past 12 years. Her siblings and their families have made the excursion north more times than we have, and her parents have logged more than 100 trips to the area since they started coming in 2006. It is a place that holds an incredibly special place within each one of our hearts for a variety of reasons, but for the same primary reason in that when you're there, you are spending quality time with one another.

We've discovered there is literally never a bad time to visit. When we go in the summer, we spend our time swimming at the pool or at Murphy Park Beach, we play golf at Alpine Resort and The Orchards, we take boat rides to see some of the 35 islands that are scattered throughout the waters of Green Bay and Lake Michigan surrounding Door County. We play tennis, we visit petting zoos with the kids, and we eat ice cream at Grumpy's until we're stuffed. We attend the best Fourth of July Festival in the Midwest right in the heart of Egg Harbor and collect as much candy as we can get our hands on before our feet begin melting into the pavement from the blistering heat coming at us from every direction, and when we're finished we walk across the street to grab a bite at Casey's and enjoy the most delicious barbeque around and wash it down with a few more ice-cold Wisconsin beers.

Colleen has participated in yoga classes on a body board in the waters of Fish Creek. Our kids have taken bike rides around the 10-mile Sunset Trail nestled within Wisconsin's crowned jewel, Peninsula State Park, and we've watched goats chew on the grass along the rooftop of Al Johnson's. We have taken a ferry from Gil's Rock to Washington Island, where we spend hours at Schoolhouse Beach tossing all-white limestone rocks into the water. Schoolhouse Beach is one of only five beaches in the entire world that are made of all-white limestone rocks, with one of the others located just a few miles away at Pebble Beach in Little Sister Bay.

We've taken trolley rides to get a more comprehensive and intimate look at unique places farther off the beaten path and discovered the gorgeous shores of Bjorklunden at Lawrence University and landmarks like Old Baileys Harbor Lighthouse, and when it was over, we watched the sun set over the water at Fred & Fuzzy's with a cherry martini. The family has spent hundreds of hours collectively on Colleen's parents' boat - *The Might As Well* - where all the cousins enjoy jumping off the massive lily-pad platform floating in the water in tow and going tubing while their grandfather drives fast & pretends to do his best to send them flying off into the choppy, white-crested waves.

And in the fall? There is no place more beautiful on the planet than Door County, Wisconsin. The roads were intentionally designed to wind in the spectacular fashion that they do to limit their disruption to the natural area and to preserve the unrivaled sightseeing that can be had when guests drive through. It never disappoints. Millions of trees, radiating a vibrance of colors that you can't find on a spectrum that dazzle the senses and leave you in awe and appreciation of the sublime vision surrounding you for miles and miles. There's nothing quite like it.

We watch Notre Dame and Chicago Bears football games on TV, and the world-famous chili dinner that Colleen's mom prepares when the family is together in Door County just tastes better in those colder weather months. We've taken the kids trick-or-treating at Halloween and been welcomed by the friendliest store owners who couldn't wait to shower the children with compliments and snacks. We've attended Sister Bay's "Fall Fest," more commonly known as "Fall Down Fest" due to the fun party atmosphere throughout the event primarily geared toward adults, where we mistakenly brought five children under the age of 7 and were the only family there with a stroller in tow. We've taken the kids sledding on the hills of Peninsula State Park's golf course in the winter, and we've gone cross-country skiing for miles across the frozen waters of Green Bay under a perfectly sunny and cloudless blue sky that looked and felt like a tangible version of heaven.

And sometimes when we're there, we do nothing at all—we just play soccer in the meadow located behind the condo, we cook hamburgers and hot dogs on the grill, the kids throw rocks into the harbor, and everyone keeps their eyes peeled to see if they can spot the humongous snapping turtle that lurks around the piers and is rumored to be older than some of the trees that surround him. Those are great days, too.

White Cliff Road is where we do most of our walking when we're together, and it truly is a spectacle. The road covers 3 miles from end-to-end, connecting downtown Egg Harbor to Juddville Road and hugging the shoreline of majestic Green Bay. The "Cliff" part within its name isn't there by accident, either—the road lies beneath the tall cliffs of Egg Harbor's Niagara Escarpment and provides some of the best places to catch a glimpse of wildlife in the area. There are deer and wild turkeys that shoot out from the brush and, on most days, you can see the remnants of a snake or two that didn't quite make it all the way across the road before having a fatal encounter with an oncoming truck.

It has been wonderful to see how much our kids love and embrace coming here. When they hear we're taking a trip to Door County, it becomes all they talk about and think about for days. They dream about eating donuts at Pink Bakery and following it up with even more desserts at The Chocolate Chicken down the street, because we're on vacation and the strict rules we keep at the house around sugary sweets get bent more and more the further north we drive. They get so excited about finding the brick with their grandparents' names on it at Harbor View Park that the family had made a few years ago as a token of our appreciation that they own and maintain a place we can always come visit. They talk about walking to the Egg Harbor Marina to snap a family picture under the same flagpole at the end of the boulder-encompassed pier as we've done so many times before.

The people who make all this possible for our family are Colleen's parents. They spend so much time and effort making sure every detail is prepared at the condo so their guests can have the best possible experience. There are stacks of containers with toys neatly organized by age to ensure there is something fun for each of the grandchildren to play with who come to visit. The toiletries are always stocked so if you ever forget to pack an important item, you feel like you're at home and the extras are only a reach away. The bedding is cozy and comfortable. There are always new games to play outside in the yard for kids and adults. Her parents are constantly searching for an exciting new Supper Club to try or setting up plans for us to visit a local attraction that we haven't been to yet. They have made dozens of day trips back and forth from Chicago just to ensure the water heater is functioning properly or to be there when the window screens need repairing or to get the front door fixed. All the details that take significant time, effort, and care to handle are always done—which is an amazing form of love for the family and for the town itself.

Not every trip to Door County is perfect, obviously. We've had to take our kids to Urgent Care numerous because they've gotten sick, we've had to cancel and cut trips short due to situations that have popped up back home, we've had crying babies who didn't sleep throughout the night that made us feel like agitated zombies for four straight days, we've gotten on each other's nerves and bickered with one another, and we've had to deal with the same frustrations that pop up anytime large groups of people gather together for a long period of time. That's life. But perfection isn't the goal, because this isn't a place that we come to once every ten years. When you go somewhere so often, it will never be perfect each time; the goal becomes more about embracing the time spent in that place, the people that you spend it with, and the memories that are made there with each other. We look back with fondness even on the trips that didn't go perfectly, because we were there together. *That's* the point. Colleen's parents are using their time and resources to bring their family together in Door County, and *that's* what matters.

To a few Door County natives who have lived in that area their entire lives, we may represent nothing but more than run of the mill "FIPs" who are just like all the other fly-by-night tourists that come and go, but I assure you we've made this wonderful place far more than a tourist destination for our family. We love it dearly, we value it for everything it holds, and we appreciate what it has given to us over the years. We look forward to being there and enjoying it together for many more years to come.

And yes, the Charles Bronson oil painting is still present in our home. It has gone through each of the six moves Colleen and I have made across the country since it came into our possession, and forever it will remain as a reminder of Door County and the Egg Harbor Miracle that occurred the first time we were there together.

CHAPTER 17

THANK YOU PAT CONROY. AND SUSANNAH.

A man I never met changed the course of my life, and I will forever be grateful for the everlasting works he created and what they came to mean to me at a time I was in unknowingly in need.

Pat Conroy is American writer—specifically a *Southern* American writer—best known to fans across the world as a master storyteller and author of novels such as, "The Prince of Tides" and "The Great Santini" which were immortalized as Oscar-nominated movies starring actors like Robert Duvall, Nick Nolte, and Barbara Streisand, to name a few.

I was not much of a reader growing up and hadn't heard of Pat Conroy or any of the movies and books associated with him until I was around 20 years old on vacation with my family in the Outer Banks of North Carolina. We had been coming to this area together for a few years by this point, and it was a place that I caught myself thinking about for weeks before and after each trip because it represented something so different from the corn-locked flatlands of Northern Indiana where I was raised, and every part of it was captivating to me.

When we would stay in the town of Nags Head, sometimes I would wake up by myself at 5 a.m. and walk down to the beach that hugged the Atlantic Ocean to watch the sun rise. As I caught that first glimpse of its glorious burning face reaching above the shoreline, I would have a hard time truly believing that it was the same sun that had provided life to me and to our planet for hundreds of millions of years. The color, the radiance, the glory of it all just seemed so much *more* when I saw it along the Outer Banks, and I could never quite grasp the words to explain how I felt when marveling at such a beauty.

Enter Pat Conroy. Enter a world of words and wonder and expression that I had no idea existed beforehand, and enter a world that I quickly became obsessed with on its discovery.

I caught my dad reading a book called *Beach Music* written by Conroy when we were on vacation that year and the idea of him being stuck inside a book left me pretty perplexed. The fact that he purchased a book and brought it on vacation or anywhere in public and was actually reading it was a sure sign that there must have been something awfully unique within those pages. Pops was not a reader, but he became entrenched in this novel and kept pulling me aside with such enthusiasm to tell me how much he thought I would like it. So, like any son trying to connect with and grow closer to his dad, I did what he suggested and got a copy of *Beach Music* for myself.

The first line of the book provides a peek into the type of journey the author will take his readers on as he highlights his wife's suicide and his family's subsequent move to Italy, all within the span of 30 or so total words. I was hooked and found the prose and dialogue in the chapters that followed so beautiful that there were sentences I would read where my eyes would well up with tears upon processing what I was taking in, which was something that I had never experienced when reading.

I'd heard the phrase "getting lost in a book" before but this felt like the opposite experience for me: this was an awakening. Reading this book and appreciating the mastery of language and storytelling that I was taking in, I noticed that I was finding out more about myself, and I wanted to keep digging to discover what else could be uncovered.

When I read Pat Conroy, I was blown away at how much life and vigor and beauty he was able to ascribe to scenes and situations that I would have overlooked or not given a second thought to. How was he able to see so much more than I did when I was looking at similar surroundings? How was he able to feel so much more and use his proficiency of not just the English language but the human condition itself to paint the type of emotion and feeling within a character's canvas that was insightful and realistic and consistent with all the sadness and joys and confusion and elation we experience as people? I didn't know the answer to these questions, but boy was I interested to try to find out.

I started thinking differently and challenging myself to create the kind of world for myself that I was reading about in *Beach Music*. "If Pat Conroy were to take this walk to the mailbox, what would he see that I am missing and how would he describe it? If Pat Conroy were to have a conversation with a stranger at this gas station, what would he try to learn about the person he's talking with?"

I began trying to extract everything surrounding me to become more aware of what I was experiencing, to make it more meaningful, and to bring myself to see it for the glorious mystery and gift that it was, even if it was the same mundane bushes I'd walked past 100 times on the same path I'd taken on my daily walks to campus to attend class. It all became an experience that I tried to squeeze the most out of for the first time, and it was a result of feeling so inspired by what I was reading. I even started writing for the first time and did my best to steadily improve my vocabulary, my phrasing, and my overall awareness to bring forth creative thoughts and ideas I hadn't thought through enough previously.

The most impressive part about how Conroy instilled this change in how I was perceiving the world was that it came from a text that cannot be considered a *lighthearted* or *easy* book to read in any sense of the word. *Beach Music* takes a vastly intimate look into hard and dispiriting issues like suicide, mental illness, divisive family relations, the Holocaust, the Vietnam War, alcoholism, and betrayal by those who are most trusted, just to name a few. These are disturbing topics to read about and think through but also ones that cannot be avoided when developing the totality of a character or a story, because of their prevalence in our actual lives.

Conroy often described himself as being depressed and "cracking" to the point of a full-out mental breakdown each time he was in the process of writing a novel, and there is no denying that the themes of his books reflect those challenges consistently. But to me, there was something so uplifting and hopeful even in those difficult emotional states and conflicted situations that stemmed from how he brought them to life with such poignancy and pain. I assumed it was damn near impossible to write out those kinds of horrifying details while still in the middle of feeling them and living through them as the author… for him to create this incredible world so effectively and vividly in his novels, I thought he had to have dealt with each of them and come out on the other side a stronger and wiser and more resilient individual.

I spent a few weeks in San Francisco toward the end of that summer and planned an entire day around how I wanted to finish reading the final Chapter of *Beach Music*. The paperback version is 800 pages, and I had made it close to the end but knew I wanted to create a special moment when completing the last pages to signify my appreciation and respect for what I had just been transformed by. It felt even more special to me because I know that Pat had spent many years living in San Francisco, and it was likely he spent time in the same places I was going to be reading his book.

I was staying with my aunt and uncle in the Haight-Ashbury District and started the day with a cup of coffee just a couple blocks from their apartment on the corner of Page and Broderick, where I took in 10–15 pages and stopped to reflect about everything I'd read in this book up to this point and why it felt so different from anything I'd read before. From there I took the train around town and made stops at Golden Gate Park, the Mission Creek Park Basketball Court, the Presidio, and finally Pier 39, where I ordered a $3.50 mini shrimp cocktail in a paper cup along with a hot green tea and finished the final page while staring out at the same Pacific Ocean that served as a backdrop within the novel and felt a sense of fulfillment and joy that remains unique and stands alone in terms of reading a book.

That was it for me; I was a lover of Pat Conroy and from there I only wanted to experience more of the beautiful worlds he had created in his books and spread the good word to the masses. What happened over the next few years was a devouring of sorts. It started with *The Great Santini,* which I connected with as a son trying to grow and sustain a relationship with a father that didn't always see the world the same way I did. Then there were *The Lords of Discipline,* which I connected with as someone who tries to maintain identity and individualism amid authoritative control; *The Water Is Wide,* which gave me the blueprint on the type of spirit and persistence it takes to make a meaningful impact as a teacher and coach; *My Losing Season,* which channeled my love for the game of basketball and the challenges and bonds that are associated with becoming part of a committed team; and *The Prince of Tides,* which left me completely awestruck by the author's ability to tell so many different stories simultaneously that tie together and unknowingly impact each other along the way. I even loved *The Boo,* which is a book Pat himself often made fun of, but I thought it was simply magnificent.

All of these books did the same thing that *Beach Music* did for me: they allowed me to find my own voice, my own connection with thoughts and emotions and the world around me in a brand-new way. Whenever I would read Conroy's books, my mind would instantly transport back to the piers of the Outer Banks, smelling a fresh pot of Hatteras Clam Chowder cooking behind me while staring out at a cloudless, crisp sky with black pelicans dive-bombing the uneven waters in search of herring, and I felt as if I was in my own little corner of Southern Heaven.

In 2008 I remember writing emails to Conroy's editor, Nan Talese, and his literary agent, Marly Rusoff, asking questions about what type of projects he was working on and when the release dates would be, and to my surprise they responded to a couple and were quite revealing and friendly when doing so. Getting an email from Nan and Marly made me feel as if I was in Pat's literary universe for the first time…to me, it was possible that one of them even mentioned my questions to him, which means that he indirectly heard from me and knew of my existence.

When I was dating Colleen, I remember taking a day off work on August 11, 2009, to be among the first people in Chicago to pick up a copy of *South of Broad* when it was released at the Barnes & Noble in the Gold Coast neighborhood of Chicago where she was living. I think it took me two days to finish reading the entire thing, likely less than that.

In December 2010 I wrote one of my favorite short stories, "My Dear Albi's Chippie," which was based on the death of my family's dog, Sophie, that I thought was the greatest dog that ever lived. The story is long and jovial and has many examples of what made Sophie so special, but at its core it is a story about the idea that love makes you better, love makes you bigger, and that the impact of that love doesn't somehow mean less if comes from "just a dog" instead of a human being. Most dog owners will attest to this, but I felt compelled to write through my own experience while also protecting the life and legacy of Sophie, because I knew what she meant to my family and I knew she was deserving of that legacy being upheld properly.

In the story I explained that the full name I gave to Sophie was actually "The Great Dog Sophie" and how I had lifted that name directly from the pages of *Beach Music*, where "The Great Dog Chippie" was a central character the protagonist Jack McCall uses when telling his precious young daughter Leah heroic bedtime stories about a dog he had growing up. Jack created a magical dog in Chippie for his daughter, and tales of Chippie's conquests always left Leah feeling safe, secure, and happy whenever she was scared or nervous about what was transpiring in the world around her.

I loved writing this short story for many reasons, and one reason specifically was that I was able to acknowledge some of the influence Pat Conroy's writing had on me as I took creative liberty and applied it to the dog I loved so dearly. From reading his books and listening to his interviews, I had a feeling this is something he would be 10,000 percent supportive of and would feel flattered by that The Great Dog Chippie had inspired the naming of other Great Dogs, but I also was never able to confirm that since I was never able to talk with him and didn't know how to contact him so he could read the story for himself.

The story was posted on a website that I created for the purpose of putting my work online so I could share it with family and friends when I felt compelled to do so. This was a simple WordPress Blog and was never something that I advertised, called attention to, or tried to gather traffic on because I was interested only in creating a medium outside of Microsoft Word where others could review the very few pieces of work I was creating at the time. The people who knew about this website's existence could be counted on one hand, and none of them, to my knowledge, ever once shared the link on Social Media sites or within other blog sites—which, again, was completely fine by me.

A decade passes from the time I originally posted "My Dear Albi's Chippie" to the blog; a website that hasn't been touched or shared or thought about or advertised or even updated for *all ten of those years*. In that time there were probably 50 million new websites created online and not one change had been made to the one I had created in 2010. Since the time I posted that story, Colleen and I had had five kids, we'd moved five times, and had countless experiences that had absolutely nothing to do with Chippie or Sophie or anything at all related to that site or those stories.

So, you can imagine my surprise when I woke up the morning of May 16, 2020, with an email in my inbox with a subject line that read simply, "The Great Dog Sophie."

Who would know about The Great Dog Sophie aside from the very few friends and family members that read that story ten years ago? And why would they send me an email about it now when the world was in the middle of a devastating pandemic and no one had a clue what was going on around them?

When I looked closer at the email and saw who the sender was, all the air was sucked out of my lungs.

"From: Susannah Conroy"

I remembered Pat had a daughter named Susannah, but why was she emailing me? And if it was his daughter and she was emailing about The Great Dog Sophie, how in the world did she find that story online when even I would have trouble trying to find it in a Google search.

I proceeded to read the email and was floored by what Susannah had to say to me. I felt so honored that not only did she somehow manage to find this story I had written in 2010, not only did she read the whole thing, but also she appreciated the nuance and message I remember trying so hard to convey when I wrote it. She *got it,* which to a writer is one of the highest and most noble goals one can strive for when creating something you're pouring a piece of yourself into.

She connected with it and understood my intention to the point that she took the time to write me a beautiful letter that I was having trouble reading the entirety of without having a heart attack when I realized it was not a fake and was indeed from *the* Susannah Conroy. I mean, Susannah was the muse for the character of the little girl in *Beach Music* and was the one who chose the name "Leah" when Pat asked her for a suggestion on the name as he was writing the book.

Beyond the wonderful sentiment the entire letter put forth, there were a couple lines she included that have more meaning to me than she could have possibly known and are sentences I cherish to this day:

"In the same way Leah embraced a dog she'd never met before as a friend, I feel much that way about you and The Great Dog Sophie."

"My dad would have loved your post. He would have been gutted by it and would have loved it even more in the gutting. The Great Dog

Sophie sounds like she was a very good girl and a very lucky dog to have been loved by The Great Human Dennis."

Susannah's letter is framed in my office where it will forever remain, located on the top shelf of my bookcase placed right in the middle of Pat Conroy's books that surround it on each side.

As I am sure Susannah and others that knew him would attest, Pat was not a perfect person. I never put him on the kind of pedestal where I needed to be disabused from such a notion. From what I have read and heard in interviews, his marriages, his relationship with many of his children and extended family members, and at times his personally destructive behaviors were examples of his shortcomings and perhaps served as the muse for which some of his mortally flawed characters are derived. But the beauty and love and life he created while alive through his work—the passion with which he led his life and the creativity he used to inspire millions of people around the world is an altogether undeniably marvelous and wondrous thing to appreciate. He is my favorite artist and author, and I truly love the wonderful worlds he brought to life for me and within me as a reader.

"Writers of the world, if you've got a story, I want to hear it. I promise it will follow me to my last breath."—Pat Conroy

I was never able to meet Pat before his passing in 2016, but to me this letter from his daughter—a woman who stands alone on her merit but is also the flesh and blood of Pat Conroy—and the words she conveyed to me mean more than anything I could have said to Pat face-to-face. Without ever meeting Pat Conroy and having the opportunity to tell him my story, I became a better version of myself through his life's work, and the gratitude I have for that will not wane as my days turn into years and I keep moving forward. I hope that my story meant something special and lasting to his daughter, Susannah, and that she knows what an impact her father—and her letter—had on me.

CHAPTER 18

FLYING IS FOR CARTOONS AND INVISIBILITY IS FOR CREEPS

CURIOSITY IS THE GREATEST SUPERPOWER IN THE WORLD.

"If you could pick one superpower, what would it be?"

Every kid has been asked this question. It's safe to assume that even before the question has been completed there are images of Spiderman's web shooting from your hands, or you next to Superman flying across the world in a flash. Every Hollywood movie that gets released these days seems to be tied to comic books and action hero reboots, so the topic is certainly finding a market within our world.

I get it.

The point of a superpower is to make you more than you are, to make you stronger, to save the day. It sucks when we stub our toe getting out of the shower or lock our keys in the car when it's freezing outside. "I bet Wonder Woman doesn't have to deal with this sh*t," you think to yourself. And you're right. Wonder Woman absolutely does not lock her keys inside her invisible jet and her toes are far too tough to stub.

That said, I've learned some good news. You don't need Thor's Hammer or Harry Potter's Cloak of Invisibility to have superpowers, change the world, or make your life better. You've just got to be curious. And commit yourself to staying that way forever.

I sit back in amazement at the natural curiosity all kids have, especially our five. Nothing makes me happier and prouder than when they ask questions. All. Day. Long. About every topic under the sun (and questions *about* the sun—which is a big point of discussion in our house). They want to know everything about what's around them, and when they find out a little bit of information, they get more curious about those details and dig in even deeper.

"Do radishes grow on trees? How many worms do you think would have I to stack for them to be taller than our mailbox? How many rocks are there in a brick?"

Even though sometimes I wish they were slightly more curious about things like, "How can I stop losing one of my shoes every hour?" there isn't a single topic that I suggest they think less about when they bring it up to me.

They pepper me with questions, and it's beautiful to witness how quickly they learn and how much their world grows, brick by brick, with each new piece of information they receive. Somewhere along the road it seems as if we lose part of that curiosity as we get older. We become afraid to let someone that we respect (or someone from whom we want respect) know we don't have all the answers. We don't want to seem weak or ignorant if we ask questions. We act too cool to be interested in something that might be pulling us toward it, but it isn't appealing to the broader group we're with at the time, so we let it go. We begin to doubt ourselves and lack the courage to think through difficult and authentic thoughts because most of the time it's simply easier not to and we instead make assumptions.

Asking the right questions and having meaningful conversations with those around you can change your life. Wherever you are in your life right now—this very second—is a consequence of every conversation you have had up to this point. Some conversations have bigger consequences and meaning than others, but every one of them has the potential to change part of your existence. Curiosity is the foundation of that.

There is risk with curiosity. I tend to ask tons of questions when I am with talking with people, and sometimes those questions are annoying to those who may not desire to have the kind of conversation that I was hoping to have. I obviously don't start with the intention of annoying anyone, and I am getting better at reining it in when I notice someone else's apathy toward what I am talking about—but I usually don't let it stop me from trying.

Curiosity helps in difficult situations. If I hear people express what I believe is a flat-out awful opinion, for example, I do not agree with them or condone the viewpoint—but a large part of me becomes curious to learn why they think that way. What experiences have they had that would lead them to act or think like that? Where did they learn to think or act that way, and why do they think it's beneficial or correct (assuming they are acting with their own self-interests in mind to begin with)? If I care enough from that point, I can ask questions to try to get a better grasp of how that sort of opinion was developed.

I don't strive to always agree with those I am talking with, but I do strive to understand what is being communicated. This puts me on the path of becoming more curious about their views rather than becoming judgmental. It helps me stretch myself mentally and remain humble, knowing I don't have access to all the earth's knowledge, so I probably shouldn't think or act as if I do.

This is not some type of new age Moral Relativism in which I think everyone and their opinions are *correct* — I just think I am able to analyze a situation much more accurately and gauge how I should react when I come from a place where I am trying to understand.

When I find myself lacking curiosity in a situation, I try to remember:

- Everyone you meet knows something you don't. Children. Homeless people. Your annoying co-worker. You can learn something meaningful from everyone.
- Even if you're the expert on a topic, there is always more to learn, and there is always room to reevaluate established truths that have gone unchecked for prolonged periods of time.
- The world is complex, and there are some very smart people and smart ideas in places you wouldn't immediately think to look.
- Curiosity is a function of gratitude and can keep you in a state of appreciation for the world around you that is full of unknowns waiting to be explored.

I believe things get better when we take a genuine interest in knowing more about the world around us, and the people with whom we interact. Maintaining a healthy curiosity about our own life experiences, our interests, our fears, and our talents, as well as those of others can be beneficial in creating a bigger, more beautiful world that you understand a little better than the one you live in when walled off by not seeking more knowledge about the environment you're part of.

CHAPTER 19

FULFILL SOMETHING WORTHY

I have learned there is real power when self-fulfilling prophecies are put into motion, and that we'd be wise to pay attention to the ways they guide our thoughts and our behaviors even when we're unaware they are doing so.

In a nutshell, a self-fulling prophecy tends to look something like this:

You hold a belief to be true. That belief impacts the actions that you take. Those actions impact others' behavior and what results from it (or your interpretation of the results), which support and reinforce the original belief you held. The original belief you held is then proved to be true and is perhaps even strengthened.

Here's an example:

- You come to the belief that a co-worker is annoying.
- You begin treating that person in a way that reflects your belief that they are an annoying co-worker.
- As a result of your treatment, that co-worker puts forth behavior that reflects the actions of someone who is annoying, or you frame their actions as annoying.

- That annoying behavior you witness from the co-worker reinforces your original belief that they are an annoying co-worker.
- You end up concluding that you were right, after all.
- Now try it this way:
- You come to the belief that the same co-worker is per-haps imperfect, but is a smart, capable, kind, imaginative, strong, confident, and resourceful person.
- You begin treating that co-worker in a way that reflects your belief that they are a smart, capable, kind, imagina-tive, strong, confident, and resourceful person.
- As a result of your treatment, that co-worker puts forth be-havior that reflects the actions of someone who is smart, ca-pable, kind, imaginative, strong, confident and resourceful.
- The smart, capable, kind, imaginative, strong, confident, and resourceful behavior from the co-worker reinforces your original belief that they are indeed a smart, capable, kind, imaginative, strong, confident, and resourceful person.
- You end up concluding that you were right, after all.

An expectation effect, like a self-fulfilling prophecy, is known as the Pygmalion Effect in psychology circles. It has been tested and proved out in literally hundreds of studies with a wide variety of subjects and circumstances and almost always arrives at the same conclusion: How we frame a situation at the beginning can have an impact on our behavior, which can lead to an impact on others' behavior, and ultimately can lead the perceived outcome of a situation to match and reinforce our initial framing. It's been proved with teachers, students, employees, athletes—it's even been confirmed when tests were set up using rats. This is a pow-erful, powerful idea with a reach that doesn't seem to have many limits.

I have learned that people tend to behave in a manner that reflects how they are treated. I have noticed that when I have positive expec-tations for the kids I am coaching or the professionals I am leading at my job, the outcome is always better. I make sure I tell the kids, "You are big, strong, and fast—I know you can make this layup, keep going!" and eventually, they come to believe they are big, strong, fast athletes who will benefit if they keep practicing. They eventually make that layup. They see someone believe in them, so they begin to believe in themselves. I don't lie to them and say, "You are the greatest player in the world," because they'll find out quickly I am not telling the truth—but I tell them I believe they are better than what they currently are (because I genuinely believe they can get there) and eventually they start to believe it themselves, which leads to them toward actions making that belief become a reality.

I have limited myself in the past by falling prey to negative self-fulfilling prophecies, too. I would say things to myself like, "You aren't smart enough to apply for that job. You don't have the right background." This would lead to me losing confidence, not putting myself out there to give myself a chance, and eventually not being selected for the role—which just reinforced my original belief that I wasn't smart enough or didn't deserve it to begin with. I eventually worked with the person who got that role and saw immediately that I was smarter and far more capable than they were, but I let my negative thoughts control my actions, so they got the role instead. Looking back, that mindset sure didn't serve me in the best way, and I missed out on an awesome professional opportunity as a result.

We all have biases to an extent, and we will frame our current environment in part based on what happened to us in past experiences. That's not a bad thing. It's healthy to know your own limitations, but it's also important that you watch what you're saying to yourself and reexamine and challenge your beliefs on a regular basis to ensure they are based on truth and strive to have enough courage to reset the course on a more accurate path when it becomes necessary to do so. You don't want to leave yourself open to getting dragged down by a negative self-fulfilling prophecy, especially one that goes unchecked and are unrecognized.

You are not God, and you will not have full control over others' behavior simply by manifesting a belief about them and treating them in a manner that reflects that belief. But the words we say to ourselves and the thoughts we keep in our minds and hearts matter. They have a enormous impact on you and those around you. Choose them carefully, choose them honestly, choose them thoughtfully, and choose thoughts that will empower yourself and those around you to impact positive outcomes.

CHAPTER 20

IT'S NEVER TOO LATE TO TURN IT ALL AROUND

"When is it too late to turn it all around?"

Colleen and I ask this question to the kids quite a bit, typically when they're in the midst of a difficult situation and they're not having the best go of it. It's usually a scene in which everything seems overwhelming, nothing is going the way they want it to, and there is no visible path in front of them that leads to any kind of improvement over their current state of distress. In those moments it is easy to feel their frustration and emotions spiraling out of control. We get it, because we've all been there and continue to find ourselves in spots just like that as we get older.

Every parent wants to help in situations like this but it's tricky—you want to acknowledge their feelings of anger or sadness or disappointment, even when the issue at hand is *only about* a missing shoe or a playdate not going well or a sibling not sharing a toy. These problems can seem trivial to adults, but to the kid going through these feelings they are very real and the issues at hand are very important. The devastation over a broken crayon can't be completely dismissed if you want to establish the kind of trust that's necessary for them to want to listen to the message you're putting across when trying to help them get onto a better path.

When the timing is right, and we've listened to what's bothering them, we come around to asking the question, "When is it too late to turn it all around?" We've tried to teach them that the correct answer to this question is "Never." It will take a little time and effort, but there are things we can do to make the situation we're in a little better.

By training our kids to think about "Never" as a response to this question, we are trying to instill in them the knowledge that they have the power to change the framing of the problem they're dealing with, that they can seek effective and creative solutions to work through it if they choose to do so, and that making the effort is better than wallowing in that storm for long periods of time, waiting for something or someone else to come save you.

Thinking through this question and answering "Never" doesn't mean that the tough situations you're dealing just *automatically* become good. But it's the conscious acknowledgment that there are small incremental changes you can make that can lead to something positive, and that's a good place to start. I think it sure beats the alternative of believing whatever bad situation or mental state you're currently dealing with is one that is destined to get worse and there is nothing you can do to make it better.

We talk about this with our kids, but boy does it also apply to Colleen and me as parents, as a couple, as employees, as friends, and as just people living in the world. When we are having an argument with each other and the tensions are escalating, the one that emerges with poise and clarity who steadies the ship back toward calmer waters usually is acting with the question "When is it too late to turn it all around?" in mind, whether consciously or not, which changes the tone of the entire conversation and creates a bridge that we can cross together to get to a better place.

When I am stuck in an uninteresting meeting at work, "Never" reminds me that I have the choice to make the best of the situation I find myself in and that there is something I can do, no matter how small, to make it better and turn it around. When I am in a tizzy with a family member or haven't heard from a close friend in a while, "Never" helps motivate me to act and attempt to get things closer to the desired state I am aiming at.

I watched the movie *Vanilla Sky* a long time ago and remembered one of the characters saying the line, "Every passing minute is another chance to turn it all around."

After I heard it, I kept repeating it over and over and over to myself, thinking how strong and beautiful and hopeful that idea was. I knew it was true but hadn't heard it phrased that way before and loved how it hit me.

In the scene, there is a painting in the background by Claude Monet titled, "The Seine at Argenteuil," which features a dreamlike eerily colored sky that inspired the name of the movie. I purchased a replica of it in 2011, and that painting has hung inside every house I've lived in since then. When I see it, I am reminded of the line in that movie and the powerful belief that while we are here, while we are alive, while we have a breath in our body, we have the freedom and power to and make things better.

It's never too late to turn it around.

CHAPTER 21

IF YOU CAN RIDE A BIKE, GO RIDE A BIKE

It may not be the "coolest" mode of transportation out there compared with a Tesla or a Ducati or some other popular brand of motor vehicle that I know absolutely nothing about, but bicycles are the greatest thing going when it comes to your ability to get from point A to point B, and nothing comes close. Even if you're just looking to get from A, then cruise around for a while with no goals or tasks to accomplish and end up right back at A, doing so on a bike is where it's at and I highly encourage anyone with the physical capability of riding a bike to do so as often as possible.

I started getting into riding bikes two years too late, in the fall of 2005. I had just moved to Chicago and didn't have many friends yet or know much about the city, so I decided to get a bike and began dedicating almost all my available free hours to exploring and learning more about the place that was now my home. Riding up and down Lakeshore Drive, tooling around Montrose Beach, learning the ins and outs of the dozens of unique neighborhoods…I was hooked, and loved every minute that my butt was on that saddle—having fun, getting exercise, and becoming an expert of the city.

I say two years too late because in 2003 I was still in college at what might be the nation's most bikeable city and campus at Indiana University in Bloomington but never once owned a bike there and never once took advantage of the trails, events, and community that was so supportive of it. Somehow between the movie *Breaking Away* being screened around campus on a regular basis and attending "The Little 500" event each spring it never occurred to me how incredible riding a bike could be, and I have no clue how that happened.

Quick tangent on The Little 500 for those who aren't familiar: The Little 500 is an annual cycling race that takes place on a quarter mile cinder-track and is held on campus every April, where more than 25,000 fans attend a 2-hour race that covers 200 laps (50 miles) for the men and 100 laps (25 miles) for the women, which amounts to the largest collegiate bike race in the United States. The event and the festivities that accompany it throughout the entire campus are what makes it known as "The World's Greatest College Weekend," with teams and riders training year-round to qualify for the chance to participate. Only the truly elite riding teams can call themselves champions when it's all said and done.

How great is the Little 500? Lance Armstrong, seven-time Tour de France winner and at one point one of the world's most famous athletes, once said, "I've attended Super Bowls, World Series, and the Monaco Grand Prix, but the coolest event I ever attended was the Little 500." And he's right. But somehow even a biking event that amazing didn't get me interested in riding during those years, and I consider that a massively big missed opportunity given how beautiful and scenic the Bloomington area is and how much bike riding is built-into the town's culture.

After getting my road legs tooling around Chicago, I started gaining confidence, getting more adventurous, and began riding my bike to work occasionally, to the suburb of Mount Prospect, 25 miles from where I lived. The first time I completed that ride to the office, using a route I'd planned, I felt so accomplished and so proud. When I finally arrived at the building, our president happened to be parking his car when he saw me approaching and yelled out, "How are you getting that thing back to Wrigley, Bucko?" I wasn't totally sure. But I knew when the Cubs had home night games and traffic was at a standstill around my apartment, I would actually get back to my place faster on my bike than I would driving my car from the office, which provided yet another incentive for me to get keep racking up the miles.

I would ride my bike when meeting my friends at bars and restaurants in the evenings, which seemed way faster and cheaper and easier than trying to hail cabs everywhere or bothering with parking your own car in a town notorious for fees and towing. I used to refer to this as the "EYB Method," short for "Earn Your Beers" at dinner, and that made way more sense than driving for 45 minutes in traffic, only to get to a restaurant and continue to sit for another 3 hours without much activity.

When we moved to Greenville, South Carolina, in 2011 everything came together for me to become more knowledgeable and involved in the cycling community. You couldn't dream of a better place for cyclists to live and ride than Greenville, which is why legendary professionals like George Hincapie, Christian Vande Velde, and Bobby Julich decided years ago to call it home. The nearby Blue Ridge Mountains offer rides with the kind of steep grades and terrain that make even the most seasoned cyclists gasp for breath and serves as a key training ground for U.S. Tour de France teams. There are more than 140 miles of dedicated bike lanes throughout the city for novices and experienced riders to enjoy.

And no list of Greenville would be complete without mention of the Swamp Rabbit Trail—a glorious 22-mile walking/biking trail that connects the city's electric downtown scene with areas as far north as Travelers Rest on paved pathways covering abandoned railroad tracks surrounded by lush greenery in every direction. It's darn near unbeatable in every way for riders and is consistently on the Top Ten list of most bikeable cities in the country. That trail remains one of my favorite places to ride a bike to this day.

Colleen bought me my first "nice bike" when I turned 30 while we were living there. For years I'd been riding whatever heavy old 12-speed or 10-speed bike I could get my hands on and was starting to put in some decent mileage without knowing what I was missing. But being the owner of an *actual road bike*, one as fast and as smooth and as beautiful as the red and black 2012 Specialized Roubaix that now sat inside my garage really opened an entire new world of riding to me, and I couldn't wait to get going.

The first week owning this new bike I signed up for my first official race, an 85-mile winding loop route that took us throughout the outer edges of town near Paris Mountain and the Greenville Watershed areas. I was less than prepared for the task that lay in front of me. Since I'd been riding larger and heavier bikes prior to getting the road bike, I never saw the need to purchase the fancy spandex gear or clip-in cycling shoes that I saw other road riders wearing in the past. Even with this new bike I was skeptical of spending money on special clothing that I thought had to be a scam to get people with disposable income to feel better about themselves while riding. I don't recall specifically, but it was along the lines of "Those posers don't know what they're doing. What a waste."

I stuck out quite a bit in the crowd of 200 riders at the starting line when I was the only person on a bike wearing a hooded sweatshirt and rugby shorts the morning of the race. "It's possible these guys know something I don't" is another thought I had as I anxiously waited for the gun to fire signaling the beginning of the adventure. I learned a long and cruel lesson that day on what the meaning of "wind drag" is while riding and paid a dear, dear price as a result of my ignorance.

To say I struggled to the finish line would be a gross understatement. Despite the crushingly poor performance I put forth that day compared with the experienced road cyclists flying by me who knew how to ride in packs, knew how to choose and wear the right clothing, and knew how to change gears when the terrain alterations called for it—I was hooked, and I couldn't wait to put in the necessary hours to get better.

When you start getting more involved in a new hobby, you begin noticing people and groups that you weren't aware existed—sometimes right under your nose—who are champions and cultivators of the activity you're now part of. It's usually a fun discovery to make and something that leads to a heightened sense of belonging to a community of likeminded folks who enjoy investing time and effort on the same things you do. I found that community in spades when we moved to Wheaton in a group of bike riders called The Rusty Chain.

This group had about as wide a range of ages, professional backgrounds, and personalities as it can get—but no one who was part of it focused on or cared about those differences one bit. If you loved riding your bike, if you loved going really fast, if you rode safely and unselfishly, and if you were up for a punishing pace to get your day started, these were your guys.

Their rides usually started around 5am and typically averaged a 23 mph pace on a 30-mile ride. They would do this 3–4 times a week and were machines in terms of their consistency and strength. I was invited to join the Rusty Chain by a neighbor I used to ride casually with and was anxious to see how I would fit in with such a strong group of experienced riders, since I was still new to road bikes.

The first time I went out with them, I got "dropped" (meaning, I fell off the back of the Peloton or line of riders within the group) after around mile 20, and I made my way back to my house alone while recovering. But rather than feeling dejected I became more excited for the opportunity to line up again the next morning and see how long I could "hold onto their back wheels."

More than just going faster and farther than I'd gone before, collectively the Rusty Chain taught me the importance of staying safe on the roads, how to ride effectively in large groups, the importance of having the right gear, and enjoying a competitive spirit when riding alongside each other. I started riding with them as often as I could, which was tough since Colleen had just given birth to our fourth child and most of my time was spent around the young family we were raising, but I cherished each time I was able to join these guys and felt as if I was becoming a pretty solid cyclist.

Beyond the standard century events (100 miles) that would take place around the Midwest that we would participate in, there were three events I rode with The Rusty Chain on that I enjoyed the most. One was the National 24-Hour Challenge (N24HC), a 24-hour race hosted in Michigan where riders go from 8am—8 a.m. on Saturday and Sunday over Father's Day Weekend to see how many miles they can knock out in one day. Cyclists bring tents and can eat, rest, and replenish as they wish throughout the day and often set up support teams, like a pit crew, so they can be met at various checkpoints to refill on food and rehydration without spending too much time off the roads. The winner of the race put in an ungodly 520 miles in one 24-hour session, and to this day I have a hard time understanding the kind of strength, endurance, and badassness that human being put forth on a bicycle.

Another fun event I participated in a couple times was called Race the Lake, which took place in Fond du Lac, Wisconsin, which circles the entirety of Lake Winnebago, one of the largest lakes in the Midwest. The best and most memorable part of this event had nothing to do with bikes or the race. Someone in the Rusty Chain had befriended a woman in her mid-80's a few years back who allowed him to stay at her home the night before the race, and it became an annual tradition that grew in attendees. She cooked dinner when we'd arrive, she cooked breakfast the day of the race, and she prepared her 1,200 square foot home as if the King of Siam was coming to visit. She was quite literally the perfect host and took such pleasure in our staying at her home. And each year following that first visit, the number of Rusty Chain riders expanded due to the unrivaled hospitality she showed the group and how easy it was to have fun and relax together at her house prior to the event. The race itself is a challenging way to explore the festive and unique Wisconsin towns around Lake Winnebago and is incredibly well-attended every year by people of all ages and skillsets.

My favorite Rusty Chain ride I ever went on was not a USA Cycling sanctioned event or an organized race at all. A couple guys in our group were training for something called the "Paris-Brest-Paris" event in Europe, which calls for cyclists to ride 275 miles a day for three straight days under strict time limits to be considered finishers. After earning their qualifying status through a few domestic "brevet" events, they had a few weeks to train for their big ride and were trying to devour as many miles on the road as possible to ensure they were strong enough to perform the way they wanted to when the time came to push through each step of the Paris-Brest-Paris. Those two men rode most mornings with the Rusty Chain, obviously, but they found that even those rides weren't enough on their own. So they developed the very cool idea to start putting in miles at a time when I certainly hadn't considered it being possible, which was at night. And from there, the "Midnight Century" ride was born.

The two who were training for the Paris-Brest-Paris had done this sort of night ride before, but most of the guys who took part in my maiden Midnight Century hadn't done it and we were extremely excited for the adventure ahead. I finished work around 5:30 p.m. that day, played with the kids, had dinner with the family, then went to sleep around 8 p.m. like everyone else in our house. I set the alarm for 11:20pm and got up, got dressed, pumped my tires, checked my gear pack, and headed toward the meeting point where ten other riders gathered at midnight to start the journey of 100 miles of backroads and farmland under the bright moonlight for the next 5 hours.

It could not have been a cooler experience for me and was something I felt so grateful to be part of the entire time because of how unique it felt and how much fun it was to be riding along other people that loved riding their bikes as much as I did. Stopping at a convenience store to grab hot dogs as a group around 3 a.m. was hilarious—cashiers working that shift are undoubtedly used to seeing some strange situations unfold at that time of night, but I'm quite sure he didn't expect ten men dressed in full spandex walking carefully around his store in bike clip-in shoes to be part of his evening. I rolled into the house around 5:30 a.m., helped Colleen get the kids going and fed to start their day, then began work in my office very tired but also feeling very fulfilled after an epic night ripping up the roads. Our two Paris-Brest-Paris riders went on to complete their epic ride to completion in France later that year and everyone in The Rusty Chain felt a sense of pride knowing that our group was represented well in one of the world's most challenging cycling events.

The Rusty Chain exemplifies a group of dedicated and skilled riders that take their love for their hobby to the next level in a variety of ways, and groups like them exist all around the world that have my utmost respect and admiration—but that kind of commitment is far from the only way you can reap the benefits of riding a bike.

Some of Colleen's and my favorite biking memories include the tours we took around the cities of Boston and Charlotte, which were conducted at a leisurely pace with tons of stops permitted for breaks, pictures, drinks, and soaking in the amazing cities in front of us. In 2013 I restored a 1979 Schwinn Tandem Bike that was actually a wedding gift to my parents, which we take around the neighborhood all the time. Every time we ride it, we think it's the funniest and most enjoyable mode of transportation we could have used when getting to our friends' houses or any restaurant that we end up at. Riding bikes with the kids for miles down the Prairie Path and through Herrick Trail are some of the best family memories we have and is always time very well spent.

Whether it's riding down the block or challenging yourself to complete a daylong double-century, bikes have something to offer to everyone and I think all of it is great. Next time you have the option, take a bike somewhere you haven't taken a bike before and reap the benefits of having a fun adventure on the best mode of transportation out there.

CHAPTER 22

A MESSAGE WORTH SPREADING

By the time you reach age 40, you should be pretty decent at detecting bullshit. You will have seen enough wayward attempts from false prophets and gurus trying and failing to start societal revolutions that don't actually benefit society, and you will have heard enough of the devious lies people spread to make themselves seem far more than what they actually are, only to be outed as con artists attempting to make a quick buck off unsuspecting victims. Thanks to a world where information flows non-stop from all directions of the globe, it can be challenging to determine the difference from what is the "truth" and what is a biased interpretation of it repackaged for their provider's benefit—but you should be much better at getting to the bottom of it at 40 compared with when you were younger.

By the time you reach age 40, you should also have a bit more perspective on how to identify those rare people out there who are genuinely trying to make things better, those who have dedicated their professional careers and their lives to a meaningful cause that brings value to society. You learn how to recognize those who are honest in their words and in their actions and are striving to make those around them stronger, more intelligent, more capable, more confident, and better equipped to carry out their responsibilities and face the challenges presented by life in a way that serves themselves, their families, and their communities in the best possible manner. You can appreciate someone who demonstrates consistent courage in the face of fire, as well as someone who brings decades of professional experience to pull from and knowledge of human history that spans thousands of years to help explain their suppositions.

You don't see too many people out there who fit this bill, because it can be a very difficult way to consistently conduct yourself. But when these people do show up in the world and you determine their intentions are true and sincere, I believe the most appropriate response is to respect their efforts and pay close attention to what they're saying and doing.

In 2017 I came across a series of YouTube speeches from a Canadian professor named Dr. Jordan Peterson and became interested in learning more about the lectures he was giving to the students in his classroom. Here was this late-middle-aged man who usually wore a tan sport coat with leather elbow patches and had greying unkempt hair and drank Diet Coke and bounced around in a dimly lit university classroom, filming himself with a camera with poor audio and zero production quality, preaching to the young adults taking his courses on Clinical Psychology that racked up views in the millions on this video-streaming platform, and at first I couldn't quite figure out why.

The more I listened to these lectures, I realized the reason his videos received millions of views had little to do with the nuances of Clinical Psychology. It had far more to do with the Master's course he was providing around the benefits of taking on more personal responsibility, on becoming a better contributing member of your communities, on becoming a better family member and friend and professional for those who count on you, on understanding and improving your habits, on building your mental toughness and overall strength as an individual, and ultimately on living a better life that benefits you and those around you.

Every clip I watched somehow seemed to find a way back to trying to get individuals to become a slightly better version of themselves than they were the day before. The more I listened, the more I wanted to learn. I cannot imagine being a student in the classroom watching these lectures firsthand and seeing this level of passion and academic competence displayed in such a manner, and not run through a wall at full speed at the end of every class ready to take on the world.

Dr. Peterson never suggests that he *created* a good portion of the content in his university lectures and on the various speaking circuits and engagements he participates in. Where he excels is taking the lessons he's learned from studying a diverse base of great thinkers and world history over the past few centuries, combined with what he's gathered from witnessing so many different facets of human behavior in his own clinical psychology practice for decades, and converting those insights into direct and easy-to-understand language that people of all ages and educational backgrounds can comprehend and implement in their lives.

He'll take the incredibly difficult and complex works from psychological giants like Jung and Freud and Nietzsche and Solzhenitsyn who usually take years to master, and compare the archetypes they encapsulate to movie characters like Pinocchio, Peter Pan, or Harry Potter to make their points easier to grasp for "normal people" without them having to study their works for years on end to decipher their incredibly important meanings.

The topics he covers aren't intended make Dr. Peterson stronger, or his political party and supporters stronger, or his opponents weaker—his messages are designed with the intention to make the individual listening to him stronger—regardless of their political or racial or gender or socioeconomic background—so they in turn can do better for those around them. This differs from the philosophy of someone like Ayn Rand, which focuses on rugged individualism and gathering power and goods for the primary benefit of the individual. Peterson wants the individual to become strong so they can in turn do better for those in their care and those around the world. He places very little value on group politics or identity politics, because he cares more about how you act and think as an individual. He tries to get those listening to him to pay close attention to building themselves into the best version of themselves, so they can do the most good in society.

After listening to dozens of Peterson's speeches, I found myself thinking and acting in ways that were undeniably better than the ways I had been operating previously, and I felt grateful to discover the message he was spreading. I began trying to speak more honestly with others about how I felt and focusing on telling the truth in all situations, no matter how awkward it might have felt. I found myself identifying when I was letting resentment control my emotions in a negative way and learned how to listen to it and mitigate it more effectively.

I started to understand my own value structure more clearly and tried to get more precise about the sources from which I derived meaning and the hierarchy of characteristics I would need to develop to get closer to the vision and aim I had for myself. I started to say fewer things that made me weaker. I started to assume that every single person I encountered knew something I didn't and became more curious to learn from them. I started to better understand the habits I had that were working against me and needed to be removed.

Was I perfect at putting any of these into practice? Very far from it. But these sorts of thoughts and ideas became more prevalent in guiding my actions, and I felt that they were leading me in a better direction as a result.

My kids have heard me repeat phrases I have learned from Dr. Peterson for a long time now and they can almost finish my sentence when they sense one coming on.

They'll hear me say "Be the fool in order to be the master" whenever they're trying a new skill like piano or math or lacrosse or making nachos in the microwave for the first time. What a powerful phrase to highlight that there can be no progress, no development of competency, no growth in anything you will ever pursue without first being awful at it and building yourself up over time. If we can be disciplined enough to embrace that uncomfortable feeling when we don't know what we're doing when we begin something new and overcome it, rather than never venturing out from what is familiar to us, growth and expansion over time becomes limitless. This saying is a reminder to be brave and humble enough to try new things—and be bad at them at the beginning—so over time you eventually improve and become the master and develop yourself into something bigger and better than you would have been without it.

My son Declan has become a decent little basketball player and has scored lots of points in lots of games over the course of his young career. But the proudest I have ever been while watching him play was when he missed 3 straight left-handed layups during a game he played in fourth grade. We'd been practicing left-handed layups together for a long time and he was getting better, but usually in a game kids will try to score with the dominant hand because they want to make the layup more than they want to risk missing with their weaker hand. On this day Declan tried a left-handed layup in a real game for the first time and the courage to do so was incredible to me. He missed the first one, but he had the gumption to try and to risk looking like a fool in front of his teammates and fans attending the game. Undaunted, a few minutes later he was on a breakaway where he attempted another left-handed layup, and again he missed. I cheered so loudly after that second miss trying to let him know I saw what he was doing and appreciated what was taking place on the floor.

In the 4th quarter of this very close game he *once again* tried to make a left-handed layup in a critical moment and he once again missed it. At this point I noticed a few parents rolling their eyes or balking that a player had missed what appeared to be three easy layups, but they never noticed that he was shooting them left-handed and was trying out a new skill during a very tense situation for a kid that age.

I don't remember if the team finished with a win on the court that day—but his true victory was having the courage to fail, to be the fool, to set himself up for future success by doing the hard thing today when it would have been far less challenging for him to do otherwise. I don't think I could have gotten my then 9 year old to embrace an idea like that so clearly without learning how to frame it from Dr. Peterson. After the game he was beaming with pride when we got together, and he said, "Dad, be the fool in order to be the master right?! Did you see me shooting with my left?!" The excitement he had in those misses was glorious.

"Be friends with people who want the best for you" is another Dr. Peterson line that Colleen and I talk about with each other and with our kids often. When you think of your friends, can you share good news with them and when you do, are they genuinely happy for you? Or do they get jealous and try to top your achievements? Can you share bad news with them? When you do, do they show sincere concern and try to assist however they can? Or do they have a strange sense of relief that things are going poorly for you, so they feel better about themselves? And most importantly, do your friends care about you enough to pull you aside and tell you when you're acting like an idiot, because they have courage and love for you and want to see you get back on the right track when you're not exactly hitting the mark—or do they just let you continue driving your car at full speed without telling you that there's a big cliff ahead that you're about to fall off because it's too awkward to have the sincere conversation? Asking these questions has helped us not only identify and keep better friends but also be better friends to those we care about.

"Responsibility is the key to a meaningful life." Don't get caught in the trap of chasing happiness exclusively because life is full of suffering, no matter which path you're on. The goal of happiness alone will not sustain you when the floods come. What sustains us during challenging times and in the face of suffering is the willing adoption of responsibility, which is the root of where we can find meaning. We can get through any "how" when we have the right "why" as our guiding principle. Aim high and continuously reconfigure your path as necessary to keep moving forward while voluntarily taking on as much responsibility as you can—whether it's caring for your family, or community, or pet, or workplace, etc. When you choose to live a meaningful life, everything you do matters—which is hard, because it means there is accountability and impact with each decision you make. When you live a life of nihilism where nothing matters, you still go through the same type of suffering, but none of it has as much meaning as it does when you're voluntarily carrying a large load of responsibility.

"Compare yourself to who you were yesterday, not to who someone else is today." You are the only person you know well enough to accurately compare yourself with. You don't know enough about anyone else's background or the details of their situation comprehensively to subject them to comparisons. The amount of money you have, your health, your physical appearance, your emotional state, etc., are a result of complicated and multifaceted factors that are not capable of being directly compared to anyone else's complicated and multi-faceted factors that make them who they are. Focus on being better, stronger, more competent, kinder, wiser, and more capable that you were yesterday, rather than trying to outdo what you mistakenly believe someone else has achieved or has reached today.

"You don't get to keep snakes away from the garden." Pretending that threats don't exist or keeping them completely away from those you care for, thereby leaving them unable to face them sufficiently when the time comes is not an act of love or kindness. If there are snakes in the garden, you should have the goal of becoming the master of snakes. Teach yourself and your kids how to deal with chaos, how to identify problems they will encounter in the world and handle them properly so they're prepared when they come face to face with them. What's better: to not be afraid, or to know that you can handle being afraid? Dr. Peterson would suggest focusing on the latter, and I agree.

After conducting speaking tours that spanned hundreds of cities and countries over the world, in December 2019 Dr. Peterson was checked into rehab after becoming addicted to the prescription drug

Benzodiazepine, which he began taking to assist with his anxiety, then suffered across every dimension of his health once he stopped taking the medication. He spent nearly two years being treated at various hospitals in Canada, the U.S., Russia, and other locations in Europe on his long road toward recovery and spent none of that time in the public spotlight. Only those closest to him knew what was happening as they went to great lengths to save his life, while also trying to assist his wife of 40 years, who was also suffering from a rare form of cancer.

He has often said that the reason he wrote his bestselling book "12 Rules for Life" was not just so others could benefit from what he's learned—he wrote it primarily for himself as a way to formulate the sort of thoughts and actions that would lead him to a better existence aimed toward not only doing less bad for the world but also putting himself together in a manner that he believed would be a positive force and overcome the malevolence and tragedy and frustrations that he would face. He never positioned himself as perfect or someone who operated without error. He was trying to share the keys to what he believed unlocked some of the troubles and challenging circumstances we all face, having learned them from his own experiences and mistakes.

I don't agree with everything Dr. Peterson has said, or done, or stood for throughout his career and time in the public eye. I recognize that he is a human being and has plenty of faults, just like the rest of us. But I have learned that you can do plenty of good without having to be perfect, and I believe that he has garnered far greater positive outcomes for those whom he has helped than negative outcomes that people have accused him of for viewpoints that they didn't agree with.

Dr. Brené Brown, an American researcher and best-selling author whose work uncovers insightful themes around shame and vulnerability and courage, is another person I respect tremendously that is trying to spread a helpful message to benefit others. I've read her books, I have seen her speak live, and I have listened to her podcasts. She would be the first to tell you that she's far from a perfect person and has made many missteps in both her personal and public life. She literally wrote a book titled, *The Gifts of Imperfection,* to highlight the ways we can better embrace ourselves and others for who we really are – imperfections and all. But those mistakes she's made shouldn't diminish the validity and efficacy of the message that she is putting into the world that is designed solely to help other people. Whether you personally like her or not, and whether you agree with her politics or not, doesn't diminish that she's putting forth real effort through her life's work with the intention of making life better for others.

It isn't easy to do in the divided social environments we've developed, but we can believe in a *message* while not wholly agreeing with a *messenger* if the message is true. Good ideas shouldn't have a political home. There is no Republican or Democratic or Libertarian ownership to a message that makes people stronger so they are able to improve themselves, their families, and their communities.

I haven't dedicated the past 40 years to treating people as a clinical psychologist would or put forth 1/1000th of the time and effort to study history to develop the ideas that Dr. Peterson has, so my ability to describe any of them comprehensively or provide an explanation of their meaning perfectly will fall far short of what they were designed to convey. But I wanted to try communicating my appreciation for the work I mentioned and what it has done for me personally since I first heard of him in 2017.

His ideas have helped me clarify my thoughts and my aim, and they've helped me understand my own beliefs and actions better. They've helped make me a better husband, a better father, a better son, a better friend, a better professional, and a better member of the various communities that I am part of. It has helped me treat people in my life better and treat myself better. I appreciate the substantial effort he has put forth to deliver these ideas to the world, despite the flaws he and other messengers like him have as individuals, and I believe the message of doing everything in your power to make yourself a better person is worth spreading for generations to come.

CHAPTER 23

NO MAN IS AN ISLAND

One evening when I was living near Wrigleyville in Chicago, I took a walk by myself and stopped by the eclectic and longstanding used bookstore *Bookworks* on Clark Street, where I stumbled across a copy of Ernest Hemingway's *For Whom the Bell Tolls* that I saw in the middle of a pile on the floor that served as an overflow device for the overstocked shelves that lined the store. I'd like to think this book caught my interest because I was such a sophisticated 23 year old looking to dive into a tragic tale depicting the atrocious horrors and destruction that come from war, but in reality I saw a title that had the same name as one of my favorite *Metallica* songs and thought to myself, "Sweet, I wonder if there is anything about James Hetfield or Lars Ulrich in here that I should know about?" And with that, I gladly paid the cashier the $6 I had in my pocket and walked back home to my apartment, hidden above a tiny law firm on Ashland Avenue, and started reading.

But it turns out that I didn't get very far at all in my reading that night. On page 2—right after the title page and directly before the beginning of Chapter 1—there was an excerpt of a famous work by 17th century writer John Donne that read:

"No man is an island entire of itself; every man is a piece of the continent, a part of the main;

if a clod be washed away by the sea, Europe is the less, as well as if a promontory were, as well as any manner of thy friends or of thine own were; any man's death diminishes me, because I am involved in mankind. And therefore never send to know for whom the bell tolls; it tolls for thee."

I must have read these lines 80 times in a row, back and forth, front to back, sideways and by-ways. This was the first time I'd come across these words and something within them just gripped me. I imagine it would have been quite peculiar if someone had been watching me that night, with my eyes staring intently down at a single page and not looking up or turning a page for what felt like hours.

The idea that Donne was presenting, the notion that people and lives of all kinds are inextricably interconnected and eternally interwoven with one another, was a concept I'd spent quite a bit of time thinking about on my own, but it certainly wasn't something I had ever been able to encapsulate as succinctly and beautifully as Donne had with this meditation. I loved the way he presented this thought and immediately felt a kinship with the analogy of being an island far away from society whenever I found myself in a deeply troubled state of mind and how hard that feeling was to process when I was filled with it.

During those times I felt sad or frustrated or ashamed about something I had done or something that had happened to me, it would trigger a sense of disconnectedness from those I was close to and even from the world at large. When that feeling hit, it was not an easy one to navigate and often led to further despair until I would eventually see the light of day and get myself back closer to center and closer with the various communities I'm part of.

I believe in the vast power that lies in spending quality time alone, and I believe in the power of individual thought. They are incredibly beneficial and paramount to developing the most authentic and powerful version of yourself. I just happen to also believe that the power of communities is equally important, and that when we spend too much time in isolation due to fear or shame or pride or spite, it doesn't serve us well and we become lessened as a result. Your family, neighborhood, school, friends, etc., all suffer as a result of your absence, as well.

I take Donne's passage to also mean that everything you do has an impact. Every interaction you have with family, friends, strangers, co-workers, etc., can provoke a change in some fashion and causes a ripple throughout your circle and throughout the universe in ways that are often undetectable and seemingly inconsequential. Even by making the intentional decision to not engage with the people around you or the communities you're part of, that decision has an impact on you and on them. You are not an island entire of itself, you don't get to choose to simply "not make an impact," because you're a real part of everything around you, whether you're conscious of it or not and whether you want to be or not. I don't always remember that, and I don't pretend to fully understand it most of the time, but it's a thought that I believe in and one that I love dearly, because it reminds me that I am part of something much bigger and my choices and actions have a significant impact on the broader world around me.

Sometimes catchy little phrases have a way of sticking in our heads to serve as reminders to seek a better route when trouble rises to the surface. Whenever I start to feel adrift or distanced from the world while in the midst of a challenging period, the words "No man is an island" pop up and lead me to the truth that whatever I am going through is temporary, and that I am doing myself and my community no favors by hiding from everyone, dealing with everything alone, and letting it linger far longer than it needs to.

John Donne's meditation leads me to feel more connected to those around me—even those I have never seen before or thought about or even been alive during the same time as. It's a call to look after each other and to recognize the many ways that we're dependent on each other to thrive in this life.

James Hetfield has written some incredible lyrics in his days as the front man for Metallica…I am fairly sure he would give a tip of the cap to John Donne and the everlasting lines he created that reminds us of a connection we share with those around us today, those behind us, and those still yet to come as part of our lives.

CHAPTER 24

CREATIVITY IS BETTER THAN DOUBT

I've been around enough children to know that creativity is a beautiful and powerful trait we're all born with and we all benefit from. And I've been around enough adults to know that creativity can atrophy to the point of near-extinction over time when disregarded, looked down on, and not put to proper use.

I feel beyond grateful that I get to stay connected to such strong and consistent sources of boundless creativity through spending so much time with our kids. What they do daily, creating and playing within their own worlds is mesmerizing and inspiring and it truly does make all our lives brighter. I hope to cultivate that a priori creativity within them and keep it alive and strong for many years to come through being an example to them of how adults can act in similar fashion and supporting their efforts whenever they are out making it happen.

This isn't going to be a chapter in which I attempt to describe the scientific hypothesis behind where creativity comes from or what impact it has on our bodies and brains. This chapter is an attempt to bring light to the courage it takes to be creative, how it should be celebrated when we come into its presence, how we all have the chance to be creative in one way or another, and how the results of bringing that creativity to bear brings more value to your life than many of the reasons we choose not to engage in such activities.

Not a ton of people I associate with today are aware of this, but in 2007 two friends and I wrote and produced a 90-minute movie based on a fictional town, full of fictional characters, that followed a completely fictional storyline we created when we were joking around together the previous summer. The project started off like everything else did when we were together, which was basically our doing the best we could to make each other laugh by coming up with the most far-fetched scenarios we could trying to get each other to break. We'd caught wind of a contest that the FX Network was putting on where amateur filmmakers were tasked with creating the funniest and most original 5-minute skit they could, and the winner would get the chance to create their own television show that would be broadcast nationally on the FX Network.

We thought this sounded like a perfect opportunity to place us squarely in the directors' chairs in Hollywood and were just naïve enough to believe we had a real chance at winning even though none of us had any particular filmmaking or scriptwriting or acting or cinematic storytelling experience of any kind that would separate us from the thousands of entrants in this contest who excelled in literally every one of those areas.

In the 5-minute skit that was created, the world was introduced to two of the most iconic characters that you've never heard of: Richard Trynowski, AKA Ricky Triceps, a local bodybuilding legend from the small town of Chivalron, Indiana, and a friendly news reporter named Bud Andrisco, a man who earned the unending respect of peers and viewers alike.

Ricky Triceps was brought to life by my friend Brady. The two of us met somewhere around 8th grade and I hated him the minute the laid eyes on him. We played on rival basketball teams in middle school and I couldn't stand how cocky he appeared every time he made a shot, which was often, and how lighthearted he seemed even in the midst of what I thought was deep competition. I was typically drenched in sweat and highly emotional on the floor, while he jogged around without a care in the world and had a constant smirk on his face and usually scored more points than I did. We went to the same high school freshman year where it took exactly two days of us hanging out together before I realized he was far more of a goofball than an adversary and we quickly became very close friends. He taught me how to take life a bit more casually than the way my competitive natural disposition tilted toward, and I was grateful for him.

Bud Andrisco was immortalized by our friend Josh, a 6-foot 4-inch silver tongued, effervescent young man who remains the single greatest storyteller I have met to this day. When we were growing up, he commanded the attention of everyone in the room – kids and adults alike - not because he was boisterous or placed himself in a position that forced you to see him, but because he was gregarious and magnetic, and you found yourself hanging on to every hilarious word that came out of his mouth even if you happened to be the person he was making fun of during his tale. Years later I introduced Josh to Colleen when we were dating and she said to me, "This guy might be the funniest person alive, but I sure hope I never get on his bad side because I don't think I could take being on the wrong end of the stories he tells as well as he does."

The plot within our skit centered on Ricky Triceps training to win a marathon that he'd signed up for and Bud Andrisco dutifully following each step of the process, reporting all the important updates to Ricky's passionate fans and admirers from afar. I was living in Chicago while this was being filmed and wasn't around much when it was produced, but I don't think I've ever laughed harder in my life than when they showed me a clip of Ricky Triceps stepping up to the starting line of a real-life race called "The Sunburst" in South Bend, Indiana, while wearing a costume that consisted of a long platinum blonde wig with curls, the shortest and tightest red shorts ever manufactured, a ripped bright yellow tee shirt, and the kind of thick mustache so concerning I am sure it caused parents to keep their children at least 25 feet away.

Ricky is at the starting line, next to real-life runners who have no idea who he is or why he's dressed like this and have no clue that they're being filmed for a skit, and as soon as the gun goes off indicating the start of the race, all that can be seen is Ricky taking off with his head tucked into his chest and his legs whizzing into a blurred dead sprint far ahead of all other participants and not relenting his pace until he is clear out of the competition's view.

How did Ricky pull this off in a real-life competitive marathon race like The Sunburst with participants that routinely break the 3-hour mark and perform at an extremely fast pace, you might ask? Well, that race Ricky participated in was a Fun Walk, not a marathon—and it consisted of mostly elderly people who were there to raise money for charity and enjoy a leisurely stroll around South Bend during a crisp and beautiful late summer morning. The onlookers were completely flabbergasted to see a grown man dressed the way Brady was and sprinting out of the gate with the fervor of a cheetah chasing down its prey, and those who were part of our film crew hidden out of plain sight could not contain their laughter for hours after seeing what took place.

Was the 5-minute skit perfect when all was said and done? Nope. Was it even good? Not even close. But it got made, and to us it was glorious. And we didn't know it at the time, but that dumb little skit ended up serving as the best possible rough draft and springboard from which more stories and creativity were launched.

It goes without saying that we didn't win the FX Network competition, but the three of us still thought our idea was hilarious and kept thinking of questions to ourselves like, "What if this really absurd development happened with Bud? What if we added this weird sidebar to the backstory with Ricky?" for the next few months. Eventually our

5-minute skit became a 20-minute script, which then turned into a 40-minute script, which eventually got so full of potential for us that we scrapped nearly everything and went on to create an entirely new storyline that we developed into a 92-minute movie. We worked on the script for 6 months and spent the next 6 months filming and editing, working to achieve the collective creative vision.

To this day the movie we created is the funniest project any of us have ever been a part of. It was challenging as hell at times and gave us the slightest sliver of insight into what professional actors and producers and showrunners and directors deal with on a daily basis to get a movie like this completed, but it was such a joy to have all of our creative synapses firing together in a manner that brought so much happiness to so many people around our hometown.

We brought dozens of friends into the mix as participants during the making of this film and at one point we had around 20 of our buddies filming a scene at my parents' house. When I did a quick scan of the room with everyone dressed in the most ridiculous-looking costumes we'd ever seen, I noticed that not one of us had a girlfriend at the time. Nobody. I couldn't tell if that was the single most hilarious realization, or the single most depressing one.

We held a movie premiere at a large banquet hall called Celebrations Unlimited in Mishawaka where a couple hundred people showed up to watch our film. We even had an article written about our efforts published in the *South Bend Tribune*. In our eyes this movie was a smashing success and accomplished everything we set out to achieve throughout the writing and filming and editing process.

All of this sounds great, right? So, what is it that could hold people back from pursuing these kinds of awesome activities and taking on more creative projects in their lives?

Well, a big one is *time*. Busy adults often feel as if they just don't have enough time in their days to pursue extracurricular creative hobbies that don't generate revenue for themselves or the families they support. And that's a fair and understandable point of view. Between jobs, social commitments, family commitments, finding time to exercise, keeping up with bills and homework and maybe getting a haircut for the first time in two months—it gets tough to find a few extra minutes by yourself to sculpt clay. I get it.

But what slows people down more than lack of time when it comes to letting their creativity shine, is *doubt*. Because once you make the commitment to yourself to carve out time in your day for creative hobbies, it becomes easier and easier to do. But doubt? Doubt is a stone-cold *killer* and is a nagging anvil that needs to be discarded if you're ever going to get away from its long and daunting shadow that keeps your creativity in the dark.

Doubt can come from anywhere at any time and can suck the soul out of any artistic impulses you have. Doubt tells you that your creative ideas are stupid. Doubt tells you that your thoughts aren't as unique as you think they are and you're not talented enough to see them through to the end, even if you did decide to try to pursue them. Doubt tells you that friends and strangers will make fun of you if you put yourself and your work out there, and the people you care about will no longer respect you once they see what you're trying to do. Doubt kills creativity and removes the power held within the mind and heart of the individual on the cusp of making something new and beautiful for themselves and the world to enjoy.

It's hard to overstate how many great moments we've experienced since making our movie in 2007 that would have been completely missed if we'd listened to all the people who told us throughout the writing and filming process that what we were doing was stupid and that we were wasting our time. We had a few staunch supporters throughout the process, don't get me wrong—but we also had many more people scoff at what we were doing and suggest that we should be spending our time pursuing other things that they deemed to be more serious or worthy or prudent or whatever—and we ignored all of it, and just kept on with what we thought was a fun and exciting and meaningful work of creativity.

If I feel doubt creep in as I begin writing a letter or a limerick or making family movies at home with the kids these days, I try to think of the fun to be had throughout the experience and the lasting impact the final outcome could have on the recipients as the way to overcome it. Why should I give a sh*t about what others think regarding the work that I am creating, if it doesn't hurt them or involve them in ways they don't accept? The creativity is something within me, something I am creating for myself or the audience for which I am developing the ideas. And sure, it would be great if everyone who saw my creation understood it and loved it, but if I understand it and love it and feel as though I honored the idea enough and gave it the level of effort and scrutiny and time to fully thrive, then that's it. That's really all that matters.

If the spirit continues to pull you that direction, go out and learn how to play that instrument. Create that poem. Pitch that new strategy at work. Cook that foreign dish for dinner. Take that acting role. Get out in nature and snap those photographs. Write your first song. Plant that garden. Paint that canvas. Hell, go out and film that full-length movie with all your friends dressed like 1980s WWE wrestlers if you feel compelled to do so. Just do something creative every once in a while, so you remember how magical the process is and feel how much bigger it can make your worldview.

Not only that, but when you see others playing that instrument or writing that poem or planting that garden—encourage them! Even if you think their performance stinks, let them know you at least appreciate the bravery and tenacity it takes to fight past the internal and external doubt they face to see their creation through to the end, which wouldn't have ever come into existence without them making the conscious decision to make it happen.

I used to write a bit more frequently before I met Colleen and had kids, and when I was really, really into an idea I remember feeling as if my feet weren't in contact with the ground throughout the day. When I wasn't writing the story, I was thinking about the story and considering all the ways I could make it better or different or more aligned with what I was trying to get across nearly every hour I was awake. It was all-consuming. There were moments I was overtaken with this beautifully odd state of panic, when I would think to myself, "Man I really hope I don't get hit by a bus and killed before I finish this story." And that is not a rational way to think, especially now with a wife and family I get it—but I remember that feeling from before, and I think it's a familiar one for those people out there who are "in it" while coming up with something creative that they're so excited to breathe into life.

I've always loved what President Teddy Roosevelt had to say when describing how much more meaningful it is to be the person who is performing a task vs. the person judging their efforts. This is another trick I use when convincing myself to have the courage to be creative:

"It is not the critic who counts; not the man who points out how the strong man stumbles, or where the doer of deeds could have done them better. The credit belongs to the man who is actually in the arena, whose face is marred by dust and sweat and blood; who strives valiantly; who errs, who comes short again and again, because there is no effort without error and shortcoming; but who does actually strive to do the deeds; who knows great enthusiasms, the great devotions; who spends himself in a worthy cause; who at the best knows in the end the triumph of high achievement, and who at the worst, if he fails, at least fails while daring greatly, so that his place shall never be with those cold and timid souls who neither know victory nor defeat."

Be the person in the arena when it comes to creative activities. Make the time and give the freedom to allow yourself to think. Make the time and give the freedom to let yourself go down the creative rabbit hole your mind opens, no matter how funny or sad or strange or farcical or ridiculous it appears to you at first. And be courageous enough to put that creative energy into action to see where it takes you.

CHAPTER 25

THANK YOU, WHEATON

Colleen and I moved to the city of Wheaton, Illinois, in September 2013 without having spent any time in the area previously or knowing a single person that lived there on our arrival. Today we consider it one of the most serendipitous decisions we've ever made for our family.

Colleen was pregnant with our third child when we were heading into the summer of 2013 living in Greenville, South Carolina, where we'd been the past two years. We had decided it would be best to move back to the Midwest, since so many of our extended family members were there and our kids would be closer to loved ones. When deciding which suburb of Chicago to live in, we cast a wide net without having much of a preference or clue as to which area would be most suitable for our growing collection of children. We looked at houses in Western Springs, Glen Ellyn, Downers Grove, Lombard, Lisle, Geneva, St. Charles…we searched pretty much all over the suburbs west of Chicago, with the goal of putting down some roots and beginning a new chapter of our lives together.

In September of that year we ended up selecting a home built in 1924 located on the Northside of town on a quiet and charming tree-lined street, and Maggie was born just a few weeks later. This was the first home Colleen and I purchased together, and we loved every part of it, right down to the original 1924 windows that performed more like tattered screens, as well as the rickety boiler system in the basement that shot wild flames out from the bottom every time it sensed I was near praying for it to function properly for just one more day.

We'd heard from many people that Wheaton was a great area for young families, and we were excited to be part of it, but when we first arrived, we didn't really "get it" in terms of what made this place special. It didn't help that we had three children under the age of 3, which kept our social options somewhat limited, or that we didn't know many people around us yet aside from a couple of neighbors, or that 2013 ended up being one of the coldest winters in Chicago's long and storied history of frigid weather. Not an ideal recipe for getting acclimated into a new area, but we were making the most of it by exploring everything around us whenever we could.

Time passed, and we eventually welcomed our fourth child, Frannie, into the family in 2015 while living in this home. We stayed on the Northside for another 18 months until Colleen was pregnant with our fifth child, Daniel, and we came to the realization that the home we purchased when we had two kids wouldn't be as sufficient for us once our fifth was born. We stayed in Wheaton but moved to the Southside of town in early 2017, into the Danada East neighborhood, which we were thrilled about because we had a few friends who lived there with young kids. There seemed to be plenty of fun activities around the area when we visited them.

Danada East was originally developed in the 1980s and now contains nearly 300 homes that are situated around a 1.3-mile loop called Hawkins Circle. There are a few cross streets throughout the circle, with various courts and cul-de-sacs, and the sidewalks that line the roads make it a dream for those that love walking their pets or taking a nice brisk stroll with their friends. When you live in a neighborhood with more than 300 homes, the odds are high that there are going to be kids everywhere, and that was exactly what we were looking for when setting ourselves up for our next home.

We learned that "kids everywhere" literally meant Kids. Every. Where. We quickly got used to hearing the constant knocks on the door with requests for our kids to play outside. Each of our children automatically added 3 or 4 best friends their own ages that now lived just a short bike ride away, and we did the same with adults whom we met and eventually became fast friends with around the neighborhood.

We made this move to Danada East just as a few of our kids were starting school, which also helped us get to know more families in town and to become more active in various events that were taking place. We'd been attending St. Michaels Church as parishioners, and our kids were now enrolled in the adjoining school as students, which marked the first time in my life that I was part of a Catholic school community. I had attended public schools my entire life, and given that Wheaton is known for having excellent public schools, I was not adamant that our children go to St. Mikes, but Catholic schools are something that Colleen and her entire family value immensely and have held dear to their hearts for decades, so we made the decision to pursue it for our kids.

I am sure that other schools our kids would have attended in the area would have been great too, but never have we been so welcomed into a community and felt such a connection to the people around us as we did right from the outset at St. Mike's School. This place became so special not just to our kids who were attending classes there every day and loving their experience, but to Colleen and me as well. I'd never had that much excitement or pride in being part of a school before, and I wanted to jump all-in to do everything I could to make the experience bigger and better for my family and those around us.

I loved that I had the opportunity to attend Mass with my kids, the students, and the staff on Wednesday mornings when my work calendar was free—that hour quickly became my favorite part of the week.

I loved sitting toward the back pews on the right side of the church, and on certain mornings when the season was just right, the rising sun would align perfectly around 8:40 a.m., and I'd get hit with an immaculate piercing light shining through the three circular stain-glass windows positioned along the top left corner above the altar. I always felt so lucky to be there when those moments would show themselves. I loved saying hello to all our children and their friends as they made their way back to class when Mass ended; it was the perfect boost to make the rest of my day great.

I loved that we had leaders like Principal Ferguson and Father Dan who set the tone for every teacher, student, volunteer, and employee in the building to bring their absolute best selves to the school and to care for one another. I loved how every morning during drop-off there was fun music blasting in the parking lot welcoming the children into school and the staff greeted each student to start the day with a huge smile and hug and high five.

I loved that during the second half of 2020 and the beginning of 2021, when other schools were fully remote or had severely limited operation due to COVID, the students at St. Mike's only knew joy and excitement and never once felt fear or a sense of loss associated with their school experience. Every single morning there was a merry band of volunteers (sometimes in coordinating Star Wars and holiday costumes to make it more fun) performing temperature checks and exuding happiness and gratitude to be there, which rubbed off on every single child they encountered. The excitement throughout the building is palpable, and it's a reflection of how much everyone genuinely loves being part of the amazing community the school has created. Everything about this place immediately felt like the best version of home to us.

I loved that we were able to participate in so many school-related fundraisers and activities to support the kids, including ones we hosted in our neighborhood. And outside the school we found ourselves discovering so much more about the city of Wheaton that we felt so grateful to have in our own backyard. We rode our bikes, fished, ran, and walked along the beautiful trails surrounding Herrick Lake near Wheaton Warrenville South High School. Our kids even dubbed one area there "Frog Heaven" which became the name we would use whenever we talked about taking a visit out that way.

We tore through the many sections of the Prairie Path, a 62-mile hiking, biking, equestrian and nature trail in Cook, DuPage, and Kane Counties that runs from Forest Park on the east to Wheaton, then branches to Elgin and Aurora with additional routes reaching out to Geneva and Batavia. That area is special to us because most of our kids started riding their bikes on the Prairie Path with training wheels and used those trails when learning how to eventually ride without them.

We began participating in dozens of different youth camps and sports leagues that were organized by the amazing team at the Wheaton Park District. We found ourselves at Seven Gables Field nearly every day and couldn't believe how beautiful and spacious the 70-acre park was. It also featured a huge playground, soccer fields, lacrosse fields, ponds, and walking trails that stretched everywhere. And when we weren't at Seven Gables, we were likely at the Community Center or Central Athletic Complex, which were home to hundreds of unique activities and events for children and adults alike. Wheaton has more than 50 parks, and I am proud to say we've been to most of them with our kids since moving here in 2013—visiting them never seems to get old or repetitive for our family. We have a great deal of appreciation toward each of them for their uniqueness whenever we're there.

Our kids started walking or riding their bikes to Rice Pool most days in the summer—another incredible gem developed and maintained by the Park District that provided some of the most fun and indelible moments of the season for each of our children that spent so much time there with their friends in the sunshine. Our kids took swim lessons there in the morning then would return home for relaxation and a bite to eat before heading back and flying down the huge rapid slides that shot people out like a bullet into a beautiful array of clear blue water the bottom.

We love the library downtown and the massive children's section in the basement, which feels more like a fun museum compared with children's sections in other libraries I've seen. We love playing and coaching in the Briarcliffe Baseball League and can walk to every practice and game right from our house because the fields are that close. We loved galloping through Cosley Zoo to feed the farm animals and eat a delicious ice cream cone at the snack stand when the adventure is over. We love taking the kids golfing at the Cantigny Youth Links 9-hole Par 3 Golf Course where they learned the game and are able to play without adults in their own foursomes with their friends. We love playing basketball at all hours of the day at the Wheaton Sports Center and taking advantage of their incredible childcare facility whenever Colleen and I needed a break to get a little exercise in or a quiet place to sit and get some work done for a few hours while drinking coffee in their lobby. We love visiting the French Market on Saturday mornings and letting the kids grab some fruits and veggies to chow down on while making our way through the crowded aisles of vendors, looking over what's for sale that day.

And if all that isn't enough, the city of Wheaton even built pickleball courts smack dab in the middle of town in 2021 that Colleen and I would ride our bikes to whenever we were able to find the time.

Wheaton was a completely dry town from 1934 all the way through 1985 and occasionally people will still ask if the Prohibition-Era restrictions remain in place today. All one needs to do to get an answer to this question is peek inside any of the booming restaurants downtown that serve the kinds of cocktails and fare that make you feel like you're right back in Chicago, but this is even better, because you're 5 minutes from home. During COVID the city closed car-traffic on Hale Street and created an amazing space for restaurants to serve customers outside under large, connected tents, which became one of the most fun places for residents to gather and relax together during what was an undeniably difficult time for patrons and service employees alike.

But more than anything, we love the people we've met here. We now have some of the greatest friends and neighbors across Wheaton who mean the world to us. They've welcomed us, they've supported us, they've challenged us, and they've made us better versions of ourselves in so many ways. We have a community of friends who watch out for one another because we want the best for each other. I love when we're at a party and I find out that someone I was hoping would attend isn't there, but it's because he's at his kid's soccer game or piano recital or he's watching the children that night while his wife enjoys a night out with her friends. Our friends are people trying to do their best and prioritizing what's important, and I love it.

Is Wheaton perfect? Not even close. Wheaton has the same crime problems and broader societal issues that plague every town across the world. But it's perfect for us right now while we're raising our family here, and we are extremely appreciative of the experiences we've had here together and the people we've had the pleasure to know.

We want to continue making the most of our experience here and build on the awesome foundation that's around us for years to come. We want to host fun events like the ODTC (O'Donnell Track Club) workouts during the sweltering summer mornings in the field behind our house for the kids. We want to continue hosting events like the Thanksgiving Turkey Trot and Turkey Bowl football games around Danada East each holiday, because it feels as if the neighborhood was designed for such fun and inclusive communal activities. We want to attend the parties and awesome music festivals and cultural events that the city puts on downtown. We want to coach the kids' sports teams when we can. We want to get our family outside and enjoy the trails, marshlands, parks, and pools that are here. We want to continue to be grateful for all the wonderful opportunities Wheaton provides for us to be together and continue to give back as much as we can by being the best friends and neighbors and community members we can be.

So, in short, thank you. Thank you to the business owners and community members who have made investments to bring this town to life. Thank you to everyone at St. Mike's, thank you to Danada East, thank you the Park District and city planners for developing an area that is so fun and accessible for children and family members of all ages. And thank you to all the incredible neighbors and friends we've met around here who have made Wheaton so special to us. We truly love this place and are grateful to be experiencing it alongside you.

CHAPTER 26

SCIENCE, PYRAMIDS, AND DENNIS RODMAN

I was a student in eighth grade science class at Grissom Middle School where the eclectic and wildly popular teacher, Mr. Dennis Bottorff, held court. His reputation was legendary among staff and students, and everyone was thrilled if they saw his name appear as one of their teachers when schedules were released each year. He was quick with a joke, always had a great comeback ready for any smart-aleck remark that came from the back of class, and had one of the most positive natural dispositions I recall seeing from an educator at the time. This is not to say he was a pushover—he was far from it and would quickly and adequately administer discipline to anyone that deserved it, but that type of approach was rarely his first trick out of the bag when trying to get a student to achieve their best in his classroom.

One of the unique things I recall about his science class had nothing to do with which type of ions contained a positive charge or how molecules were formed. All that stuff was nuts to me anyways. Instead, it had to do with reading. Mr. Bottorff's class lasted 90 minutes due to the new "block scheduling" our school implemented, which meant we had fewer classes per day but each one lasted much longer than before. Mr. Bottorff had a pretty strong hunch that 90 minutes straight spent talking to 13 year olds about science and science-only likely wouldn't get any of us very far. So he broke up the class into three different periods to make it more interesting to the students, thereby increasing their willingness and capacity to learn. The first 40 minutes were spent on science, and the last 35 minutes were spent on science…but the 15 minutes between would be used for reading. Students could bring in a book on any topic that interested them, as long as they focused on reading throughout the time they were supposed to and not messing around with other activities.

I always enjoyed these 15 minutes, not so much because I loved reading (because at that time I certainly did not) but since I didn't really love science no matter how good of a teacher Mr. Bottorff was and the time offered a needed reprieve for me. One day I brought in a book to read written by one of the most popular NBA players in the league at the time, and I couldn't wait to crack it open during the middle of class. The author of this book played for the Chicago Bulls, he was fresh off winning another NBA Championship, and he was an iconic global superstar—so of course I thought his book would be absolutely appropriate to read at school.

If you're trying to remember which book Michael Jordan or Scottie Pippen wrote that year, I will spare you the trouble. Michael Jordan and Scottie Pippen did not write books that year. Instead, the book I brought to Mr. Bottorff's class was authored by Dennis Rodman. It was titled *As Bad As I Wanna Be,* with a cover that featured the athlete with dyed hair and tattoos all over his body sitting naked on top of a Harley Motorcycle with nothing but a basketball covering his private parts. I was petrified of girls when I was 13 years old and reading salacious details about Rodman's exploits with the likes of Madonna and others was not going to be very helpful to me, so I am not quite sure what I thought I was going to get out of this book, but I brought it to class nonetheless.

Mr. Bottorff noticed the book I was reading and asked me to come out to the hallway with me so we could talk. He didn't do this in a threatening or mean way at all, so naively I had no idea what he wanted to discuss as I was heading out of the class with him.

"What are you doing reading a book like that, Dennis? That stuff is garbage, c'mon. Where did you even get that book? You can do better than that, right?" he said.

"I don't know," I replied." I really like basketball and I think he's cool. It's not that bad."

"It actually is that bad for a kid your age, and you don't need to be reading it. Tell you what…if I give you a different basketball book, will you promise to read it during class? I will let you borrow it, so you can take it home, then you can return it to me when you're finished, and we can have a quick chat about it."

"Sure, I guess. Do I get to keep reading what I brought in today though?"

Mr. Bottorff stared coldly at me in silence, and that look said all I needed to hear. I walked back into the classroom and placed the book to my backpack before grabbing a *National Geographic* magazine to flip through for the 8 minutes remaining before the science lessons started again.

The next time we had class, Mr. Bottorff met me in the doorway and handed me the book he'd promised. It was titled *They Call Me Coach* by John Wooden.

"If you like basketball, this is the best person you could learn from. Enjoy."

I'd heard of John Wooden and knew of the incredible success he had as the head coach at UCLA a few decades prior, but I didn't know anything about his personal life or the broader philosophies he used with his teams. I certainly wasn't expecting Mr. Bottorff to give me a book on Coach Wooden when he told me he had something basketball-related in mind for me, but I was committed to giving it a shot during the reading break in class that day.

I cannot communicate anything biographical on Coach Wooden that hasn't already been written or told by tens of thousands of people on his behalf, but I can say that I was blown away when learning more about him reading this book. One of the things that immediately fascinated me was Coach Wooden's ties to the state of Indiana. I couldn't believe that he was born and raised in the same state I was, or that he played college basketball at Purdue University, where he was the first three-time consensus All-American, or that he spent nine years coaching high school basketball at South Bend Central in the late 1930s and early 1940s. I'd spent my entire life around the South Bend area—how in the world was I not aware of that fact? Why didn't our town have statues of John Wooden on every corner or name every single boulevard in his honor? These were pressing questions to me as I continued digging deeper into his story.

I finished the 350+ page book in less than a week. I don't remember many specific details about the teams he coached or how many accolades he or his players picked up along the way, but I do remember being struck by the way he described the relationship he had with his wife and how important their marriage was to him. Coach Wooden met his wife, Nellie, when they were freshmen in high school. Before every game he played in high school, he would find Nellie in the crowd playing cornet in the band and lock eyes where they'd give each other the "OK" sign to show they were both ready to go, a tradition that continued throughout his entire coaching career.

They were married in 1932, raised two children, and had a beautiful relationship in which they kept each other as their main priority throughout their life together. John and Nellie probably spent more time together on the road at games and events than any college basketball coach and spouse in history, according to those who were around them. Wherever John went, Nellie came along as his confidant, his best friend, his champion, and his partner through wins, losses, and everything in between.

When Nellie passed away from cancer at age 73 in 1985 after more than 50 years of marriage, Coach Wooden's dedication to her seemed only to grow. On the 21st of each month, he would visit her crypt in the mausoleum where she lay to say prayers next to her and would write her a love letter. When he was finished with the letter, he would untie the yellow ribbon that was wrapped around an envelope that contained other letters he'd written and place the new one inside. Then, he'd retie the yellow ribbon and place the envelope along other meaningful artifacts under the pillow Nellie used to sleep on in the home where they lived together.

I learned that he loved poetry and would regularly create aphorisms to bring life to the complex feelings and thoughts he was working through in his mind. I learned that despite his immense popularity across the sports world, he too had to deal with people who didn't agree with the way he ran his program and regularly accused him of cheating to get an unfair advantage when it came to recruiting. I learned that he received a seven-point creed that was given to him by his father on his graduation from elementary school, which included:

1. Be true to yourself.
2. Make each day your masterpiece.
3. Help others.
4. Drink deeply from good books.
5. Make friendship a fine art.
6. Build a shelter against a rainy day.
7. Pray for guidance and give thanks for your blessings every day.

But what I learned most about—the one thing he is perhaps most widely known for among the many impressive reasons he is remembered—was the Coach Wooden Pyramid of Success.

Coach Wooden spent many years identifying the common characteristics, behaviors, and traits that he believed defined successful people, and in 1948 released these qualities within a triangular diagram that he called the Pyramid of Success. It has been said that Coach Wooden originally designed the Pyramid as a teaching tool for his players, but the work contains no references at all to basketball, or any other sport for that matter, and never once mentions anything about

UCLA. Instead it serves as a roadmap to become a better and stronger human being, no matter your background or occupation or skillset.

What the Pyramid does that is so unique is highlight what I believe are indisputable characteristics, placing them in a very thoughtful order to demonstrate how they build off one another when people are acting in a manner that generates strong, positive, lasting outcomes. You may dispute whether Coach Wooden is the best messenger for this type of thought exercise (though few would) but the characteristics themselves that he calls out seem rather unimpeachable to me. It would be hard for anyone to convince me that traits such as Integrity, Patience, Poise, or Initiative are in and of themselves a bad thing. What the Pyramid does so effectively is to bring attention to them, so we don't forget about their importance throughout the minutiae of our days, and we put them all together to live in a better way. No one could argue that Self-Control or Reliability are wrong—but we tend to not think about or remember traits like these when we're moving too quickly or not paying attention to our intentions, which thereby causes these traits to fall by the wayside in our actions. Awareness impacts action.

Coach Wooden starts at the cornerstones of the Pyramid—Industriousness and Enthusiasm—Industriousness because there can be no substitute for hard work and proper planning, and Enthusiasm because one must truly enjoy what they're doing and brush off all the detractors they will face to obtain worthwhile results. From these cornerstones Coach Wooden moves across the base of the Pyramid and up one level at a time, continuously building on the traits, with those he deems as "mortar" on the sides holding everything together. At the top of the Pyramid stands the characteristic Competitive Greatness, the ability to be at your best when your best is needed (which is every day) and the genuine enjoyment of a difficult challenge.

And what then of Success? After all, this diagram is titled the "Pyramid of *Success*"…what did Success mean to Coach Wooden? It's the best definition I have heard and is one I try to keep in mind on a daily basis:

"Success is peace of mind which is a direct result of self-satisfaction in knowing you did your best to become the best you are capable of becoming."

To me, the best part about this idea of Success is as much about the words that are *not* present in the definition—words like Winning, Popularity, Championships, Wealthy, Status, etc.—as it is about those that are present. Everyone can strive toward this version of success, no matter what goal they're pursuing, and candidly I believe it's the version that we all *should* strive toward…if you've truly dedicated yourself and gotten the absolute most out of your abilities, what else could there be? The peace and satisfaction you receive from knowing you truly did everything you could to become the best version of yourself is everything — once that's complete, the results will fall where they may and almost become a secondary concern compared with the process.

Most of the ideas presented within the Pyramid weren't "new" to me as I was reading the book and thinking about each of them more deeply…of course I had heard of Cooperation and Sincerity and the like, but never had I seen them captured and presented the way they were in Coach Wooden's Pyramid. I was mesmerized by their simplicity, their straightforwardness, and the way the traits intertwined when placed together. I imagined being in the locker room getting instruction from him as a coach and getting the feeling that his intentions were not limited just to improving my game as a player to contribute toward accomplishing our team's goals, but improving who I was as a person and setting me up better for lifelong success by listening to and following actions of a man like Coach John Wooden.

Coach Wooden was a principled, disciplined man who operated with humility, someone who took his role of coach, teacher, and leader very seriously, and someone who remained a mentor to his players long after they stopped playing on his teams. He always held the belief that the journey is better than the end. He was in his 16th season at UCLA before he won his first title (very few people know or remember that fact) and will be the first to say that the journey from that first season at UCLA in 1948 through the tenth championship his team won in 1975, the relationships that he formed with those he cared about—and the way he impacted the lives of thousands of players and coaches and fans for decades—were worth more than the hardware that came along at the end.

Looking back, it isn't as if Dennis Rodman had *nothing at all* of value that I could have learned had I continued reading his book un-interrupted in eighth grade science class. But I must agree with Mr. Bottorff's opinion that Coach John Wooden had more to offer that 13-year-old boy when it came to developing guiding principles that could be understood and applied to my own life in better fashion than what I would have gathered from Dennis Rodman at the time. I give Mr. Bottorff so much credit for caring enough to interject a different book in that situation—for caring enough to put my mind and heart on a path that would serve me better, and for caring enough to hold me to a higher standard than what I was holding myself to. At age 40 that sort of impact is what I strive to have when I see younger kids making decisions that aren't best for them. Mr. Bottorff is the example I think of if I ever need the courage to show someone that I care enough about them to try and help and redirect.

About a decade after that eighth-grade class I purchased a children's book called "Inch and Miles" an illustrated story by John Wooden written as a rhythmic poem that breaks down the Pyramid of Success in colorful, easy to understand ways for young kids. The story features an Owl as a teacher (Coach Wooden) who gives his two pupils (an inchworm named Inch and a mouse named Miles) one final assign-ment before their summer break – to define success. So off Inch and Miles go on an adventure where they encounter different animals that highlight and explain various components of success that come from the Pyramid.

I purchased this book before I had kids and before I'd even met Colleen. I was curious how Coach Wooden would communicate the ideas within the Pyramid to the youth and I was not disappointed when I thumbed through the book for the first, second, and tenth time after receiving it and picked up a few new things I'd missed from the original book Mr. Bottorff gave me.

I still have a copy of "Inch and Miles" at our home and have read it to our own children, who quickly gravitate toward the themes and grasp the important messages Coach Wooden communicated over the course of a career and life that spanned nearly 100 years. My kids have a framed copy of the Pyramid of Success hanging in their bedrooms, and it reminds me that Coach Wooden's impact goes for beyond the players he was able to lead as Head Coach of UCLA—he is one of those rare few that have an impact on anyone that comes across his work—and we're all better for it as a result.

CHAPTER 27

THE POWER OF A PRAYING MOTHER

I don't know of many forces in the world that are more powerful than that of a praying mother. I've seen it. I've felt it. And I remain unconvinced anything else out there quite matches its impact.

We didn't attend church very often when I was growing up, and I didn't know much about any particular denomination or religion, but I knew that I had a mother who prayed for her family, because I saw and heard it in action on a constant basis. It started out simply enough with my mom reciting prayers to me at night before I would go to sleep and progressed into different forms as I got older. What began as "Please help my son make some friends while away at daycare today" when I was a toddler evolved into more of a "Please God, help me from beating my son to death with a shoe if he gets in trouble with his friends again," approach during middle school and high school, which was certainly warranted.

No matter the age or circumstance, my mom's first instinct was to pray about whatever was taking place with her family as a way to obtain assistance and guidance, so she could be supportive in the best way she knew how to at the time.

Can't find your keys? "Pray to Saint Anthony!" Stressed out about an upcoming test? "Be joyful in hope!" You get the idea.

Your kids never get to an age when concern ceases as a parent. You will forever worry slightly every single time they leave your sight, no matter how old they are or how capable they are or how safe their conditions are or how strong your faith is. And as my siblings Shannan, Knute, and I got older, my mom would throw something resembling a prayer at us almost every time we left the house, asking God to look over us and protect us. I truly believe she was asking God to do so when she would say this to us out loud, but I also think she was trying to remind us that we had a mother who sincerely cared about what we did and that we should act accordingly when going about our business in the world.

When we would stumble and hit a difficult place in life, she would pray for us to have courage and strength to bounce back quickly, but more importantly she would pray that we remember that no matter what happened we had a mom who loved us unconditionally and that it would all be ok. That sort of safety net is so beneficial for a child to feel because it gives them the freedom to try new things, to make mistakes, and know that they would never lose the most important thing they've got in their lives.

When we'd have success and find our way through to an achievement we'd been pursuing, she'd pray that we remain humble and give the glory to God who provided the strength and wherewithal to make it happen. That message always reminded us that it's critical that we spend time practicing, training, and controlling what we can to put ourselves in the best position to win—but at the end of the day, everything that occurred was a result of God's will and blessings that fell upon us.

As we came into adulthood, her prayers shifted to her children discovering a career that they would enjoy and excel in. And far more frequently than that, she also prayed that her children would exhibit the sort of behaviors and attitudes that would attract the right life partner when the time came for such a thing to take place.

My mom would be the first to admit that prayer alone in no way promises a path without conflict—Lord knows she's dealt with more than a few challenges that were not avoided despite her consistency in prayer. Like anyone else, she faced demons she had to fend off throughout her life, there were traumas she overcame from growing up in a family that experienced quite a bit of conflict. There were job losses, health struggles, frustrations, disappointments, and losses of dear friends. She did an incredible job of being there for us *always* throughout these challenges, but to say anything came "easy" for her wouldn't be truthful at all, given how many obstacles there were for her to work through.

And if you ask her, my mother would tell you it was prayer and prayer alone that helped her get through all of it. It was prayer that allowed her to work up the courage to get a nursing assistant license at age 58 when she was looking for more stability and consistency in her days. It was prayer that allowed her to be such a special force to so many of our friends who came through our home growing up and allowed her to represent a consistent source of love and light even when she wasn't feeling 100 percent mentally or physically. It was prayer that helped her become the best possible version of herself and transform into the dedicated and amazing grandmother whom she turned into when our children were born, making our kids' lives far better and more meaningful than they ever could have been without her. My mother has driven more than 25,000 miles back and forth between Osceola, Indiana, and Wheaton, Illinois, to spend time with her grandkids over the last ten years and has become an integral part of their childhood.

It was prayer that gave her the strength to let go of relationships that were no longer serving her best interests. It remains prayer that helps her stay so supportive and loving to her family when we need someone to listen or give us a hug, and it's prayer that has helped her love everyone around her in such a big way because it keeps her focused on what truly matters in life. I couldn't be prouder or luckier that I have a mother who prays for those she loves, and I have seen the incredible impact it has had on her life.

When I hear and see Colleen praying for our family, which she learned to do by listening to her own mother praying when she was younger, I know we're in the best possible hands, and it makes me grateful that our kids get to feel that same source of power that I did growing up.

Even if you're not a mother, or you don't have a relationship with your mom, or if your mom is no longer alive, I believe you can still pray with her in mind, and the power of your intentions will grow exponentially because a mother is connected to it.

When moms pray for their families, there are no Jewish Prayers or Christian Prayers or Muslim Prayers or Agnostic Prayers or Wiccan Prayers—all there is is a woman whose heart is exploding with gratitude or fear or excitement or hope or sadness or joy or anxiety—often a combination of all these and more—trying with everything she has within her to provide solace and support and guidance and wisdom and love for her children and her family. And if you ask me, there's nothing more beautiful or powerful than that.

YOU ARE MORE THAN YOUR JOB TITLE

The career you choose to pursue and the success you attain within it can have a pretty significant impact on a multitude of aspects of your life. The work you do can have an influence on the overall fulfillment you feel at times, it can have an impact on the type of lifestyle you will be able to support, it can have an impact on your community, and it can create a few of the social circles of which you will become a member. You will spend an inordinate amount of time, effort, stress, and dedication working at your job, and whatever endeavor you choose is no trivial matter. Work is an important aspect of your life to pay attention to and shouldn't be taken lightly.

But I have learned that the job you perform does not solely define your value or potential as a person, and it would be wise to not tie the entirety of your identity into the professional title you happen to hold at any given moment.

When you work 40, 50, 60+ hours per week at a job, it's easy to understand how your sense of self could get lumped into the job you perform. As an adult, you are going to have plenty of weeks when you spend more time with people you work with than the people in your family and perhaps times when you're on the road for work more than you're at your home. There is a strong sense of pride and accomplishment when you're achieving professional goals, which can boost your self-esteem and even raise your status among your peers as you demonstrate competence and responsibility and ultimately attain success in your role. All of that can feel really, really good and is worthy of pursuit.

But the affection you receive from those you work with is often conditional and hinges on you doing something valuable for them to feel that way about you. It is usually transactional. What can you do to accelerate someone's career development and get them to the next level? What can you do to help the group hit their targets? If you can assist with these things, people you work with will provide the affection, title, compensation, power, profile, etc., you're striving to obtain—right up until the point you no longer can do so.

When people lose that job, that title, that compensation, that profile, I've seen that their identity can be lost along with it, and that can be a lonely and dark place to find yourself in if you've tied your sense of self-worth to those conditional things. The type of work you do can say *something* about you, but if you find that it's telling the entire story of your identity and personality, it may be time to step back and consider an alternative framing.

Arthur Brooks is a behavioral scientist and author who has spent a good portion of his career studying happiness. He is professor of a class at Harvard titled "Leadership in Happiness" and, among other insights he's provided, he teaches that the key to happiness relating to work/life balance in large part revolves around the investment in non-transactional relationships.

One of his suggestions is to prioritize "Real Friends" over "Deal Friends," or those clients and partners you work with that are there only for financial incentive or reward. There is nothing wrong with having a wide variety of Deal Friends—anyone who has worked can quickly convey how critical it is to develop a supportive network of professionals whom you work with to achieve the goals you're pursuing to help each other along the way. But Brooks suggests that longer-term happiness and overall satisfaction comes from the presence and depth of having Real Friends—the family and people that care about you and will stand alongside you and provide assistance and love and enjoyment with nothing to gain for themselves.

If you feel that the work you do or the title you have is the primary way you identify yourself, it can be helpful to focus on the "why" behind your work, rather than "what" it is you do in your job. "Why" ties into goals and vision you have around what you care about in your life, like supporting your family or serving your community or providing a benefit to the broader society. "What" is just the means by which you get there and often gets conflated with ego and the reliance on professional titles.

My "what" has changed over time and will continue to change as I develop my career—that part has never been my passion—but it's a tool that helps me achieve the goals I have within my "why," which is always around providing for my family and learning as much as I possibly can about the people, businesses, and industries that I am part of, to become most effective.

I care a great deal about the work I do. I pride myself on leading and developing a strong, cohesive, and highly capable team when I am at my job. We trust each other, we help each other, and we care deeply about each other. But I make it a point to never call the group I lead a "family" because it cheapens what family means to each of us, and using that phrase is disingenuous. Acting like you *truly love* the people you work with and will be there for them through a lifetime of challenges like family doesn't strike the right chord to me and isn't an accurate way to frame what is happening.

Coming together to become a truly good team at work is challenging and meaningful enough when executed the right way—likening the workplace to family isn't accurate to me because if you lose a job, your company will work on replacing you immediately, and healthy relationships with family members simply will not act the same way.

I've talked with people approaching the end of their career and asked what advice they could provide given all they learned and experienced throughout their time working. These are people who have had highly successful professional lives and have done extremely well for themselves, their families, and their communities. Most of the time their advice sounds like a version of the following:

"Prioritize time with your spouse and your kids."

"Prioritize keeping up with your health."

"Prioritize maintaining relationships with the friends and people you care for."

At no point has anyone given advice to me that included dedicating your entire life to drive bottom-line results on a P&L for a company you're associated with. Or sacrificing bonds with your family in exchange for a promotion. Or leaning so heavily into your work that you lose focus around the aspects of your life that can provide deeper and longer-lasting meaning.

The work you do is important. It doesn't matter if you're an accountant, a teacher, a CEO, a dishwasher at a restaurant, a dog walker, a bus driver—people are relying on you to do a good job in your role. By putting in sincere effort in whatever job you're performing, you acknowledge your job's importance within society, which can provide a sense of fulfillment even in the most menial of tasks.

Everyone has bills, everyone has to eat, everyone has financial obligations to meet that require money—work is often not a choice. But Brooks says what *is* a choice is how we look at ourselves: defining oneself as a work machine and deriving self-worth from that can be "a recipe for dissatisfaction, even misery."

You are someone's child. You may be someone's sibling. You may be someone's father or mother. You are someone's very dear friend. You play a critical role in the many communities in which you exist, and people need you. I've learned it's best not to fall into the trap in which these crucial pieces of you become hidden or tossed aside as you're carving your path through the professional world.

You are more than your professional title. You are more than your compensation. You are more than the status and perks and adoration that come along with it.

You are more than your job.

GOOD DAYS VS. BAD DAYS VS. GREAT DAYS

Another phrase Colleen and I say around the house frequently with the kids has to do with how we mentally frame the challenges that pop up in our daily lives.

We try to keep this idea simple, since our primary audience is still grasping the whole "tying their own shoes" thing and opts more toward the "I know you said it's bedtime, but I am going to ignore what you've been saying for 45 minute and start playing LEGOs instead" approach. Simple also works for the two of us, because a phrase is sometimes easier and faster when we need to remind each other and be on each other's side when we need an assist.

The phrase is "Good Days vs. Bad Days vs. Great Days," and I believe only one part of the phrase actually requires explanation.

You know the Good Days. The train is on time. Your work meetings go smoothly. Your partner is thrilled to see you when you get home. You have plans to eat at your favorite restaurant that night. You receive several fun and supportive texts from your family and friends where they let you know how much you mean to them. It's even raining just slightly, which makes the walk home from the restaurant with your partner that evening a memorable and romantic experience that the two of you will remember for years to come. The whole day from start to finish is nothing short of blissful.

You also know the Bad Days. The train is on time, but you forget your computer at home, so you have to turn around, which causes you to miss the train. Now you're going to be very late. Since you are late, you miss the super-important meeting you were supposed to lead, which causes the project to go severely off-course and makes your team grow frustrated with you and perhaps makes them think you're unfit to be in this position. You come home extremely agitated from a hard time at the office and snap at your partner for no good reason at all, which makes them cancel the dinner reservation you had at your favorite restaurant and instead send angry texts to you explaining all the reasons you were being a jerk unnecessarily. And it's raining just slightly, which makes you incredibly sad when you look out at the window and wonder why you haven't seen the sun in what feels like weeks. The whole experience seems like a calamity of epic proportions when you're in it.

When Good Days are present, the best possible thing you can do is soak them in and enjoy them and be grateful that they are there. They are *glorious*.

And when the Bad Days come, recognize that there's just no avoiding the fact that you're going have them pop up from time to time. They're awful. And you will get through them.

Great Days for us are different and are the ones that I thought worthy of deeper explanation to the kids. Great Days are more than just really, really, really Good Days. The equation is not Good Day + Ice Cream = Great Day. Great Days are even better than that. Great Days are when things go wrong, when you face huge challenges, when you're in the midst of what is shaping up to be a Bad Day, but you're able to *overcome* what's in front of you and turn it around and make it into something positive, productive, meaningful, and better than where it was heading before you made the choice to take small steps to improve it.

We don't sugar-coat or ignore the bad and difficult things we encounter. I don't think that's a helpful approach, especially when you're leading the emotional development of children who need to be exposed to the entire spectrum to sufficiently grow—but I want our kids to learn that the bad things you come across in a day or week or life don't have to break you, don't have to stop you cold, and don't have to take over the rest of your day. It's ok if they do from time to time, and those are Bad Days. But you can overcome bad things, and when you do, it's far more powerful and meaningful and fulfilling than not going through anything challenging at all.

We appreciate and enjoy Good Days together.

We help each other get through Bad Days together.

We *celebrate* Great Days together.

We celebrate Great Days, because the conscious and courageous choice you're making to willingly look at whatever is staring you down and take it on with strength and resilience, hoping that it will get better, is worthy of praise and is worthy of showing someone that you think what they're doing is admirable.

Now, the equation Great Days + Ice Cream? Nothing is better than that.

CHAPTER 30

THERE ARE NO SHORTCUTS TO ANY PLACE WORTH GOING

I have worn an electronic abdominal belt as a substitute for running in the attempt of sculpting my stomach, and I have hurriedly flipped through the Cliff Notes version of *Macbeth* the night before I was due to present a 10-minute oral presentation in class the following morning. Both events have something in common that I learned the hard way: taking shortcuts never generates the same results as putting in the work toward a task at hand.

No meaningful goal or pursuit that is truly worthy of your time and efforts and skill and presence has a shortcut to its destination. We seem to grasp this concept pretty easily when we look at a world-class concert pianist performing their craft—the dedication and sacrifice it takes to reach such supreme competency seems so obvious, so clear, so telling— you get a visceral understanding of the devotion and hard work that is necessary to develop mastery in an area like this when you watch them play and create the beauty that comes forth from their fingertips. The thousands and thousands of hours spent struggling and fighting and learning and improving—there really is no faking it. There is no shortcut. There is no path around—the only way to get to a destination like that is "through."

But we tend to forget that the same concept applies to our own lives in ways that have nothing to do with artistic or athletic performance. If I want to build a strong and loving relationship with my spouse and family members and friends and community, there aren't any shortcuts available if I desire to do so in a way that breeds authenticity and trust and long-lasting results. I must show up for others and demonstrate care when it's needed on a consistent basis. It doesn't take perfection, obviously—but it does take effort, and they must know they can count on me to be trusted as someone who wants the best for them. This takes time and hundreds of micro-interactions that build on each other to grow into something strong and wonderful. There is no elevator. It is a journey of ten thousand little steps. And when you take the long way to get there in a pursuit like this, the journey and the destination become far sweeter.

If I want to build a successful career, there aren't any shortcuts available that will provide the kind of fulfillment and output that would come if I chose instead to dedicate myself to working through all the challenges I encounter along the way and make myself stronger in the process. You may think you're helping your career by taking a shortcut and lying on your resume to get that new role or being dishonest to the bank to get that loan, but if you're not competent to do the job well or lacking the resources to pay off the loan, the results will eventually show and you'll be in a far worse position than one in which you proceeded with full integrity. You also won't experience that glorious sense of accomplishment that comes when you truly *earn* something; instead, you'll have the empty and shallow feeling that comes when we cheat to get ahead.

Shortcuts are everywhere if you're looking for them—you must make the choice whether you want to take them, and it can be more difficult to make that call when you're in a challenging situation. I have taken shortcuts—I have cheated on tests to get a better grade in middle school and high school, and when I received an A on those assignments, I didn't feel particularly good. I robbed myself of the reward that comes through putting in the work. I have also taken the long way in various pursuits throughout my life, and I have always benefitted most when I took the way through.

It's a shortcut to settle for less than you deserve. It's a shortcut to follow the crowd instead of what's inside your heart. Those are choices that are made to create less resistance. But every notable goal we pursue is riddled with resistance in one way or another. Taking on the challenges with honesty and excitement about the fight is what makes accomplishing the goal the sweetest. It's not about speed or cutting corners; it's about putting forth your absolute personal best and honoring the goal by not cheating it. If you've read any children's adventure book ever published, the theme remains the same: To get the gold, you must first slay the dragon.

Nothing is given. Put in the work. Embrace the struggle and the journey. Thrive within the improvement process. Don't cheat the goal, and don't cheat yourself by taking a shortcut.

CHAPTER 31

UNPACK YOUR BAG

Think about how challenging it is to run a marathon, to climb a mountain, to lead your family effectively, to perform well in your job, or to accomplish any of the big goals you've had your heart set on for the past few years. These types of efforts take a tremendous amount of vision and hard work and commitment to do them well, and they require the totality of your presence to deliver the desired results. Even under the best of circumstances, with the proper support systems in place and getting all the breaks throughout the process, big goals and big tasks are a humongous undertaking that demand everything you've got if you want to do them correctly and get the most out of whatever it is you are pursuing.

Now, imagine taking on any of these Herculean tasks while lugging around a massive bag that creates irritation and pain for the carrier whether you're moving or standing still. Imagine that it's an old bulky bag with a broken handle which makes it hard to manage and seems to only get heavier the longer you carry it around. Imagine that instead of making your muscles stronger as a result of carrying this weight over time, each step you take with it makes you weaker and less able to handle the responsibilities and pressures that come along with pursuing the meaningful goals you are undertaking.

Carrying that bag around would make you far less excited to show up and perform those tasks and would likely contribute toward you delivering some pretty awful outcomes compared with you taking the world on without it. That bag and all the weight within it would slow you down quite a bit.

So, the question is, who in their right mind would decide to willingly carry around such an unnecessary thing and constantly add more weight to it when it is obvious that leaving that bag behind would be so much more beneficial for you and everyone around you and would lead to better results?

Unfortunately, this lesson has taken me nearly every single one of the 40 years I've been alive to painstakingly grasp, and it's one that I hope I continue improving on and implementing in more ways as long as I live, because I've discovered it is critical to the outcome of everything I pursue.

I am not proud to admit this, but I can be a pretty stubborn person at times, and I can become too competitive in situations that just don't call for it. I have a tough time letting things go when I feel wronged and have a bad tendency of framing things in a "zero-sum game" fashion in which there is one winner and one loser when facing a situation. I have a long memory which at times fogs my vision and causes me to see more of the past, instead of the present as clearly as it appears.

This is definitely not a good thing, mind you—it's not something I am bragging about and is something I am always trying to improve—but I've been myself long enough to recognize it. Over time I started to realize that I have paid a significant price for this mindset in the past without having a clue that it was me holding myself down and adding weight to a bag I didn't even know I was carrying around and making my life far more difficult in the process.

If I got into an argument with Colleen, a friend, a family member or if I got short with my kids or one of my coworkers—rather than quickly apologizing for my actions and moving on, I would sometimes avoid the topic in hopes that it would be forgotten about without needing to revisit it or for me to apologize. I thought that if I let enough time go by, they might see my side and believe they were truly the ones who were wrong in the situation, not me, and there was nothing that needed to be done on my end to rectify whatever had become cracked in the process.

When those same people would treat me in ways that I thought were unfair or rude, I would hold it over their heads even after they apologized and not forget about the situation in hopes that I could bring it up again in the future (sometimes years down the road) and they would remember that I was right in that moment and they were wrong.

This was nothing but me acting like a jerk, obviously, and unknowingly adding a weight to my own life and to those around me which over time began creating a vicious cycle of more frustration, more arguments, less enjoyment, and less ability to take on the important responsibilities I was pursuing at the time in the strongest and most capable manner that I could. Had I handled those situations in a more constructive manner, I would have been able to work through the initial frustrations and come out of them a stronger and lighter person because I would have been unloading most of the burdens that were weighing me down.

When my daughter Evelyn was preparing for her first reconciliation at school in second grade, our priest, Father Taschetta, provided a similar analogy that the kids grasped and responded to immediately. He asked for a volunteer and selected Evelyn to come to the front of the church where his demonstration was taking place. He asked Evelyn how light and carefree she felt on stage with nothing in her hands, and she quickly agreed, not knowing what was about to follow. He then proceeded to hand her four trash bags filled with garbage, and when he asked her the same question again, she admitted that her lightness and carefree spirit took a bit of a dip when she had to carry around these garbage bags while in front of the congregation. Evelyn asked where she could put them down, so she could get a break, and it was at that moment that the priest connected her letting go of the garbage bags with attending confession and letting God take care of the bags from there.

Father Taschetta explained that those garbage bags were filled with sins and misdeeds and they are a considerable burden to us and those around us when we don't take care of them properly. The same principle applies to adults. We add weight to our bag when we hold onto grudges. We add weight to our bag when we actively choose not to forgive those who have acted against us. We add weight to our bag when we don't ask for forgiveness from those we know we have wronged.

We add weight to our bag when we allow resentment to stir within us and take over our psyche rather than having an open, truthful, respectful conversation with those we need to have a talk with to gain clarity. We add weight to our bag when we hold onto feelings of shame that stem from thoughts and actions that may have taken place weeks or decades ago that cause us to feel as if we are somehow less worthy of love and respect and care and friendship today.

We add weight to our bag when we gossip and speak unkindly about others; when we lie and cheat, even if no one else notices it; when we take each other for granted; when we exploit or suppress those around us; and when we treat those we interact with as if they are not built in the image of God. There are endless ways we can add weight to our bag that hold us down and lead toward a path of darkness.

We remove weight from our bags when we provide an honest and sincere apology to those we've wronged—an apology that is authentic, that acknowledges the specifics around how you messed up and the impact it had on someone else, and that includes the intention not to do it again. We remove weight from our bags when we provide forgiveness, even if the person who wronged us isn't necessarily seeking it or deserving of it.

We remove weight from our bags when we acknowledge that everyone around us is dealing with stresses and pressures and challenges that we have no idea about and offer grace to them instead of a harsh, quick judgment at their first misstep.

We remove weight from our bag when we work honestly and diligently toward a meaningful responsibility that benefits you and those around you, when we speak and act with kindness, and when we provide service to those around us. There are endless ways we can remove weight from our bag to free us to live in a stronger and kinder and more loving fashion.

Life is hard enough, no matter sort of extensive resources you may have at your disposal or how many friends you've got or what your job title is or whether you have five kids or no kids or you're married or you're divorced or single or young or old—there is no path out there that is easy once you decide to sincerely care about the responsibilities you take on and care about the people around you. Every single route you can possibly pursue will undoubtedly present its own set of challenges that you will need to be completely present for if you want to take them on in the best way.

The bag we carry will always have some amount of weight to it, because that's what responsibility and reality represents to an extent. But we don't need to make our lot in life worse by choosing to add the heaviest burdens out there, like wrath and jealousy and resentment and choosing not to forgive when we also have the choice to let them go instead. These awful emotions will sneak into your bag from time to time; it's darn near unavoidable as someone living in the world and being human. But when you notice yourself more exhausted, more frustrated, more pessimistic, or more hopeless than you know you could be, take a look around that bag and throw out those things that are weighing you down.

CHAPTER 32

I JUST DON'T CARE WHOM YOU VOTED FOR

This might seem like a shocker in the year 2022, so prepare yourselves, but here it is: Whom you vote for does not make you a good person or a bad person, and it does not make you a person better than or worse than someone else who voted for a different candidate. Even if you decide not to vote in a local or national election, that singular act does not make you a good or bad or better or worse person than those who did decide to vote.

(Steps down from soapbox)

With rights come responsibilities. You have the *right* to vote, so you could argue that there is a *responsibility* to exercise that right by voting for the people you think would do the best job representing your personal, collective, and/or national interests in the manner you believe to be better than the alternatives.

There is a plethora of challenging issues plaguing our society that are worth speaking up about to drive positive change and require your fighting spirit. The world has always been beset with awful tenets like oppression and inequality, and as long as we live in a society that is susceptible to the negative aspects of human nature those will unfortunately continue and will need to be addressed through social and political action from those willing to be courageous and make the change.

What I have learned is that when trying to get your point across and trying to persuade others to join the movement you're committing to, however, is that the approach "Be Tough on Issues, but Kind to People" tends to get the best results and avoids the gross personal insults that don't move anyone closer to the side you're trying to get them on.

I was in the middle of my first month of my freshman year in college on September 11, 2001, a date that changed the trajectory of the world on a macro-level in innumerable ways forever and altered the path of my university experience on a micro-level. I became obsessed with learning more about why and how an event like this could happen. The classes that gripped my interest from that point on were primarily focused on the way governments, nation-states, and militant groups interacted with each other on a global stage. I certainly wasn't interested in these sorts of topics before September 11th, but throughout my college experience I couldn't get enough of this information because it consumed nearly everything being felt and discussed around me in the world and ultimately led me to major in Political Science.

And looking back, I was just the wooooorst. Absolutely insufferable. There wasn't a single conversation where I didn't attempt to throw myself directly into the middle and project a sense of knowledge and superior insight, turning every discussion into a political debate just to hear myself talk and repeat things I'd either just learned in class or heard on cable news television. At age 40, I cringe for that young kid who was trying to demonstrate that he had an opinion, but didn't understand that the performance he was putting on was one based primarily in vanity; these conversations I was engaging in couldn't have been intended to actually persuade others, because what rational person would change their mind after being talked to as if their beliefs were not worthy of respect and thoughtful dialogue?

Time went by and I didn't stop caring about political topics; I just stopped caring about trying to convince anyone of anything that they didn't want to believe in the first place. And magically, my life and my conversations around these topics got much better.

I still care very deeply about the direction that our country pursues. I have strong feelings on a variety of political topics, and I know that how we elect our political leaders is one especially important way that our collective direction is set.

But I also believe that in addition to voting, the most important thing you can do to influence the direction you believe to be best for the country to take is to live in a manner that you believe to be worth following. That way, if others like what they see and want to emulate your way of thinking and living, they have the right to do so, or not to do so. Demonstrating virtuous actions and ideas to start whatever political or social movement you prefer is better than *trying to force* others to join you and is superior to publicly shaming others to join you—especially those who may differ in vision.

So, in a sense the title of this chapter is wrong. I do care about whom you vote for because I think it's an important way that our country moves forward. But I care far more about how we engage in the conversation around the topic with each other. I care that respect and open-mindedness remains present during the interactions people have with each other on the topics, and that we don't ascribe broad moral virtue to any individual solely based on whom they vote for or don't vote for.

I care about how we speak to each other and how we treat each other. I care more about focusing on what we have in common with each other as human beings instead of any political differences we may have. There is a reason that topics like abortion and gun control and immigration have been debated nonstop for decades on end without anything ever being fully resolved—these topics are complicated! People are complicated! Life is complicated! These are not clear-cut binary issues, no matter how strongly you feel about either side. When someone disagrees with your point of view on these sorts of topics, it doesn't automatically mean they're an idiot or that you hold the key to unchallenged truth that applies to all reality. Take a breath and strive to understand before you go crazy.

I have many Democrat friends and I have many Republican friends and my favorite part about them is how little the topic of politics is discussed. We're too busy talking with each other about what's going on in our marriages and our kids' lives and our jobs and working to support each other and being there for each other. I would never be friends with someone solely because they agree with my politics, and I would never not be friends with someone who disagrees with my politics. I think that would be a poor and shallow way to select friends and would not attract the kind of people I would want to hang out with anyways.

CHAPTER 33

THE GREATEST BOOK
EVER WRITTEN

Sure, sure, sure…Leo Tolstoy wrote a couple of pretty good books during his run as an author.

So did Dostoevsky and Hemingway and Dickens and Austen and Wilde and Steinbeck, I guess. They were fine.

If you have time, some people suggest they would be decent authors to read if you happened to be interested in petty things like expanding your worldview in ways you cannot possibly fathom or obtaining a better understanding of the depths of the human condition. Simple.

But if you have the time or desire to read only one book, I wouldn't recommend anything from lists where their books are prominently featured.

The one I would suggest is "Have You Filled a Bucket Today?" by Carol McCloud. If you haven't heard of it, that's ok—the good news is that you could ask most 7 year olds you come across and you'll likely get a colorful and comprehensive overview of what they have learned from it and ways they are applying it to their lives. It was originally published in 2006 and has since been taught at schools and daycares and youth centers across the world with millions of copies in print and countless workshops and seminars focused on it.

The idea behind the book is incredibly simple: everyone in the world walks around carrying an invisible bucket. You can fill a bucket by showing love to someone, when you help someone, when you say or do something kind, when you express gratitude and appreciation, or even when you give someone a smile. When you fill someone else's bucket, you simultaneously fill your own bucket, as well.

When you hurt others or make fun of someone or say and do mean things to others, you dip into their bucket and take out part of the good that was in there and simultaneously do the same to your own bucket. People feel happier when their buckets are full, and they feel sad and lonely when their buckets are empty.

I love this book so much because it inspires easily understandable ways to take action. It brings awareness to the thousands of mini-inter-actions we have with the world around us daily…you start to grasp just how many opportunities there are to do small things throughout your day to make someone else's day better along with your own. Filling buckets quite literally makes the world a better place, and you can be the person who makes choices to get it closer toward the environment where kindness and love are more prevalent. There are so many factors that can impact a day and a life that are out of our control—but there are so many more that are within our control when you break it down into the smaller and simpler ways your minute-to-minute, hour-to-hour, day-to-day life is structured.

Yes, being heroic and saving another person from a burning build-ing would be obviously considered a "bucket-filling" type of exercise—if you can do so it would be great to execute and help someone so clear-ly in need of your assistance in a situation like that. But "bucket-filling" could also mean being patient and giving a smile to the young fast-food employee struggling to understand how to use the cash register, and saying thank you sincerely to the teacher spending so much extra time and effort helping your daughter learn a particularly challenging subject at school, and giving someone your time when you know they're having a difficult day. You will encounter far more opportunities to fill buckets that at first appear to be small, but by approaching them with intention and recognizing how impactful they can be to others you're interacting with, you start to see the tangible power and potential held in each one that can be unlocked if you enact upon them accordingly.

Do you love someone? Good. Go tell them and tell them why you love them. Is there a friend of yours whom you respect or whom you find inspirational? Awesome. Let them know. Do you have a neighbor who appears lonely that you could go check on and say hello? Sweet, go do that. Then see what happens in all these situations.

The beauty of the book also lies in the accessibility of the message… kids of all ages can grasp the concept quickly and usually can identify fun new ways they can begin filling buckets. It is all so very *simple*.

With life experience, however, you quickly find out that "simple" does not always equal "easy." The idea behind this book is *simple* in that it provides a clear and understandable way you can make a positive difference in your life and in the lives of others. To do so on a consistent basis, however, can be beyond difficult and takes a lion's share of discipline to learn how not to react to each of the potholes surrounding you that seem to be begging you to bring forth a "bucket dipping" type action in response.

There is no chance that humans are ever going to be capable of acting in a bucket-filling manner 100 percent of the time. That's where the great novelists and storytellers really become valuable. Tales from the Tolstoys and Dostoevskys are so timeless and appealing not because they paint a rosy picture of perfect human behavior and emotions and experiences—quite the opposite. The great novelists can lay out various ideals that can be strived for, then highlight the multitude of ways their characters fall wildly short of them and rise again on their long and arduous journeys. The beauty for great novelists lies in the pain, in the struggle, in the great misdeeds of human beings…it is the tale of what takes place before, during, and after someone dips directly into a bucket, figuring out why they would do such a thing, and how those actions impact the broader world within them and around them.

We need great novelists like those mentioned who can create great tales of struggle because we too will spend a large portion of our lives struggling. By learning from these deep thinkers, we can better understand what we're up against and become more capable of demonstrating the strength we will need to tap into when the situations call for it.

But we also greatly benefit from authors like Carol McCloud, people who can take a complicated concept like spreading goodness and love toward others and turn it into a lighthearted and memorable story that people ages 4 through 84 can understand, believe in, and put real action into. That is not an easy goal for any writer to accomplish, but I think she nailed it and I am grateful for what she created in such a beautiful book from which we can all learn.

CHAPTER 34

WINDOWS, DOORS, AND RUGBY TOURS

The community where I grew up was a football factory when I was a student.

I didn't have a ton to do with this as an individual contributor, but during my four years of high school we went to the state championship three times and won it twice. The players and coaches who were part of our football program were 10,000 percent dedicated to developing the team to be the absolute best it could be, which meant extensive practice times, weight training, and film sessions during the season, and it also meant all those activities and many additional ones during the off-season. Football never really stopped for us, which became prominently clear when we would line up against our opponents.

Normally I would have transitioned right into basketball season in November of my senior season, but I was feeling burned out for reasons I cannot specifically recall and just didn't want to play on the team. So, I talked with the coach and decided to not tryout. To this day the decision not to play basketball for the school that year—choosing *not* to play a game that I had a passionate obsession with and had dedicated 20,000+ hours to practicing and improving and loving since I was old enough to walk—strikes me as an incredibly odd one when I look back at it. Was it my own emotional immaturity and inability to take harsh direction from a legendary head coach who was notoriously disciplined and structured? Was it the difficult realization that I wasn't talented enough to reach the goals that I had for myself as a player? Was it the desire to have some free time after school for the first time since fifth grade, instead of running off to a practice or game or workout session? It was very likely a combination of all those factors and other subconscious ones, but it was a decision I made nonetheless.

Had I played basketball in the winter that year, there is unequivocally zero chance I would have allowed my friend Chris Shelley to drag me to a rugby practice that spring to play a new sport that he'd been quietly becoming one of the best players in the nation in over the previous four years. Chris was talented enough at football that no coach could threaten to limit his playing time or his stature within the team if he decided to play rugby each spring, and even if they did, Chris had the kind of self-assured mindset that I'm not sure it would have bothered him if they did. He found out as a freshman that he loved playing rugby, and no one was going to tell him otherwise or discourage him from doing so.

After a long winter feeling regretful about my choice not to play basketball and spending time watching my best friends play a sport that I loved and watching them make it to the state championship for the first time in school history, I gave in to Chris's demands when he told me that I was playing rugby with him in the spring. I went to my first practice to meet our team's head coach, Bart Bottorff.

Coach Bottorff had started this rugby team six years prior to my joining and was working through the bureaucracy of administrative obstacles that our school required to get a club activity off the ground. There would be little to no funding provided by the school, since it was a club sport. For training or for games, we were not able to use most of the fields that were owned by the school. Obtaining buses for away-game team travel was nearly impossible, getting a student trainer to help with taping and injuries and such was not a common occurrence, and due to the prominence of other school-sanctioned sports taking place in the spring, Coach would often have a hard time finding a consistent group of players to field a full team.

None of these issues ever deterred Coach Bottorff or his staff at all. He'd been playing rugby for nearly 20 years leading up to this coaching position. He was very familiar with the challenges associated with growing and developing a grassroots campaign with limited resources, so in his mind this was all run-of-the-mill type stuff that he expected when engaging in the sport of rugby in the United States in the year 2001.

Watching Coach Bottorff operate was inspiring to me because he spent *so much* energy and time and expertise coaching the basics of this new game to our team, which in itself was a monumental task for a sport very few Americans knew anything about or were able to play before college at the time. But to see how undaunted he was throughout the constant ankle-biting non-game related challenges like those mentioned previously really demonstrated to me how much love he had for the game and his deep commitment to giving back and creating an opportunity for us to learn. I felt incredibly lucky to learn the game from a guy like him.

The more I learned about rugby from Coach Bottorff, the more I fell in love with the game. I couldn't believe how different the somewhat stoic culture of rugby was compared with football culture and basketball culture, where in-game celebrations and self-congratulatory displays were so common…those things just didn't happen in rugby, and if it did, it was universally looked down on by players and spectators alike. There was an unbreakable expectation of respect when you set foot on the pitch—respect for yourself in how you played the game, respect for your teammates, respect for your opponents, respect for the referee—there is one only person on the team even allowed to *speak* to the ref during a match and at no point did the conversation ever become filled with insults or slurs or backtalk between the two, no matter how heated or frustrated either side was. How different is that compared with watching an NFL or NBA game on TV?

I loved how self-regulating the game is. If there was ever a dirty play or unsportsmanlike conduct, it got handled during the match by the players, and the referee would often take the side of those protecting the spirit of the game. I loved that there is a genuine need for team-work—no individual, no matter how fast or strong or skilled, can effectively take on 15 opponents alone, and you learned that sometimes it's better strategically to go to ground when you're carrying the ball while you have support instead of pushing ahead for an extra 5 meters by yourself like running backs do in football. I loved that you play both offense and defense throughout the game, that everyone has a chance to carry the ball and contribute in so many ways no matter your size or body type, and that overall endurance is seen as more important than brute strength alone, since matches are 80 minutes long and the most effective players are often the ones who can play hardest over the longest period of time. I was never terribly impressed with players from other sports that could bench 600 pounds but couldn't run a quar-ter-mile without being completely gassed, and those types of players didn't seem to fare particularly well when playing rugby.

When I would watch professional rugby matches played by teams like New Zealand and South Africa and Ireland, I noticed that their head coaches were rarely on the sidelines during the match. They sat away from play with their staff in something akin to a media box or suite and instead let the players determine what needed to be done on the field. The idea behind this was simple but so beautiful to me: the coaches believed their job was to get the team as prepared for the match as they could, to train their team to the best of their ability before the match took place, and to help make every individual on the team play to the best of their individual ability. As soon as the match started, the responsibility to play the game, to execute the plan, and to obtain favorable results fell squarely on the players who were on the pitch. I loved every part of that thought process.

The best thing about that first season playing with Coach Bottorff was that I was able to bring my 8-year-old brother Knute with me to a few training sessions and matches so he could get his first taste of the sport and see what kind of liking he took to it. There weren't many 8 year olds around the United States aware of what rugby was in 2001, let alone many 8 year olds out there actually *playing* rugby, but Knute was one of them, and boy did he take advantage of the opportunity. Knute had been exposed to every other sport that most American kids played up to that point and found his interest to be tepid at best in each of them. But rugby? This was a sport he seemed born to play and he quickly shifted his free time away from activities like baseball and soccer over to improving his rugby passing skills and practicing his running lines even when no one else was around to play with him.

I enjoyed the experience of playing for Coach Bottorff so much that I went on to play the following fall when I enrolled at Indiana University. Over the next 4 years Knute was able to attend a few of my college matches and it allowed him to see a different level of play, but more importantly it gave the two of us a strong connection and a shared interest that we could discuss frequently together while we were apart and when he was at such a young age. My coach, Sarasopa "Sopa" Enari, was someone I looked up to and respected immensely, not just as a rugby instructor but as a man and mentor at a time when I needed one. This was a guy who had decades of playing experience growing up in Samoa and knew more about the sport than anyone else our players had met before. When he wasn't coaching, he served as a church minister and did amazing work throughout the Bloomington community with extensive charitable volunteering. I thought Sopa was a great, great man and I loved playing for and learning from him just as much as I did Coach Bottorff.

While I was playing in college, I started understanding the kind of bonds that are forged between teammates and coaches and opponents that I'd heard so much about when I first started. It's hard to overstate how much truth there is in the rumors that get spread about how inclusive rugby culture is around the world, how strong the comradery is, and how deep the ties of friendship extend that are formed when playing alongside others. If you were to walk into the locker room of any rugby team in any country, you would be certain to find a group of the most eclectic and wide-ranging backgrounds imaginable, especially at the Adult Men's Club level. Rich people, dirt-poor people, bankers, janitors, teachers, lawyers, doctors, quiet personalities, loud personalities, even louder personalities, Americans, foreigners, players of varying races and religions and creeds, people who have played for 15 years, people who started playing last month. Somehow, magically, none of these differences seem to matter much in the locker room in the sport of rugby, as long as you love playing and try your best to play the right way. You become connected to those around you in ways that differ from any other experience.

I learned that post-match gatherings are a big part of the culture, where the home team hosts the visiting team with food and drinks to socialize and get to know each other after the game. This sort of thing is almost unheard of in other competitive sports, but it is a regular event within the rugby community. It promotes the idea that you can battle vigorously against your opponent with every intention of fairly destroying them within the rules of the game throughout the match, but when all is said and over with, it's OK to treat each other like friends and be welcoming/respectful/gracious toward each other and not hold onto any of the grudges or anger that might have resonated while playing. That struck me as the sort of thing that could be adopted in other parts of our lives.

When I was a senior playing for Indiana, I served as our club's Vice President and had the chance to talk with Mark Cuban a few times, the world-famous owner of the Dallas Mavericks and Shark Tank television superstar. Before all those impressive titles found him, Mark was simply a rugby player at Indiana University, and whenever he would show up for alumni matches or other rugby-related events with us, that's the only kind of person he wanted to be while there. When he was at our house hanging with his teammates from the 70's, nobody treated him like the billionaire business mogul that he is in his daily life; they treated him like the guy who taught disco-dancing lessons and opened a bar in college called "Motley's" who loved to party and have a blast playing rugby with his friends.

For someone like me who was 21 years old and trying to figure out my next step in life professionally, it was very cool to see someone *that* successful not get too big for their britches or forget about the humble roots that helped develop him into the person he eventually became. We saw how much the club meant to him and his friends, just like all those former players who showed up from years past. We saw that Mark loved this club as much as we did, and maybe more —because he was the one who wrote a check for $300,000 my senior year to allow the rugby team to have a new field to play on with the kind of beautiful new lighting that allowed us to host night games on a gorgeous flat terrain that we'd only dreamed about previously.

After college I took a couple years off before joining the Chicago Lions in late 2007 and was met with an entirely different experience around what it means to play rugby at a high level. This was one of the most competitive and accomplished rugby clubs in the country, and it was quickly apparent that they had world-class athletes who were dedicated to building on the team's foundation of excellence that had been laid from hundreds of amazing players and coaches over the previous five decades.

When I say "world-class," I want to be clear that's not hyperbole. The team is consistently littered with collegiate All-Americans. Dozens of Chicago Lions players have earned "caps," which signifies the number of official games a player has appeared for their national team competing against another national team, which speaks to the caliber of players this club attracted.

The United States national rugby team is called The Eagles, and two players from my team were selected to the 2007 Eagles team that participated in the IRB Rugby World Cup hosted in France that year. Not some prominent regional championship or even national event— the actual World Cup played internationally every four years. And with two players being represented, the Chicago Lions did what any great club would do in that situation and organized a two-week tour around France to attend a few of World Cup matches to support their teammates and enjoy a bit of the countryside together on buses and in hotels and dive bars to have an adventure. I had never been to Europe up to this point in my life and being able to go with a group like the Chicago Lions to watch rugby and even play in a few local matches that were set up by the organizers of our tour was nothing short of a dream.

We had a match in the city of Toulon against a local club inside the stadium that the "RC Toulonnais" team plays in, which is part of the Top 14 League as well as the Heineken Cup. This would be something like coming to America as a group of tourists and having the ability to play a football game inside Soldier Field, and it was an amazing experience. We were hosted by another team in Bayonne that was led by a mountain of a man named Richard Tardits. Richard was born in Bayonne in 1965 and was a player on the French Junior National Rugby Team before trying his hand at American football as a walk-on at the University of Georgia, where he became a star defensive lineman. Tardits went on to play in the NFL for four seasons and then came back to France, where he was a member of the 1999 French World Cup Rugby Team. Tardits was our liaison when we stayed in Bayonne. We played a match against his club on a gorgeous sunny afternoon before attending the post-match celebration at the Bayonne City Hall building, where we met the town's mayor and enjoyed hours of food and drink, getting to know this fantastic group of men better throughout the evening.

Being part of the Lions for the 2.5 years I was there was another great experience I was able to share with my brother, who was now older and far more skilled at rugby than he was when I was playing at Indiana University. To be able to bring him on some of the road trips and have him get to interact with these talented players and watch the game played at a higher level than he'd seen before was special for both of us. To see him asking other players questions about their technique and reviewing ideas together was so cool for me, because you could just sense that he was picking up every piece of information that was coming across and would put it to good use as soon as he got on the pitch back home.

By the time Knute started playing rugby in high school, Coach Bottorff had transformed his club into a perennial national powerhouse. Gone were the days of wearing mismatched uniforms, scrambling for bus rides, and having a difficult time scheduling an opponent. Rugby around the Midwest and throughout the nation was on a rocket ship compared with the state it was in ten years before. Every part of Coach Bottorff's program reflected that positive change in 2010. His teams were fully equipped with the best practice gear, the best assistant coaches, the best trainers, and the best parent support system anyone could ask for.

As part of the vision Coach Bottorff had for expanding rugby's growth across the Midwest, he had spent years securing and developing a piece of land 10 miles away from the school that he completely transformed into the most pristine pitches around. This new area, The Moose Rugby Grounds, became the crown jewel of rugby throughout the entire Midwest and would be used by his team for home games as well as for various regional and national tournaments that they would host.

The transformation of a program was complete. All that was left to do for his team was to play the game and win—and win they did. Knute went on to win multiple Midwest Championships playing for Coach Bottorff in high school and he did it the right way, the way any rugby player who loves the game would respect. He was a spirited leader who always helped his teammates play to the best of their ability, he was the hardest worker around, and he was the most unselfish player on the pitch whenever he laced up his boots.

Knute eventually received a scholarship to play rugby at Davenport University, where his team won the 2011 USA Rugby Division 1 National Championship and the 2012 D-1AA National Championship, and finish as runner up in other National Championship tournaments in 7's. From there Knute went on to play for the Austin Blacks Rugby Club in Texas, where he would become a stalwart on their team for nearly a decade, excelling at an extremely high level. He was part of the inaugural "Austin Elite" team that participated in Major League Rugby (MLR), which represents the highest level of professional rugby the United States has to offer.

The state of rugby in America today is strong and is in far better standing than when I started playing in 2001. The United States was recently named the Host Country for the 2031 and 2033 World Cup events for men and women, and that kind of progress can be attributed to people like Coach Bottorff and Coach Enari and thousands of coaches just like them who have dedicated their time and expertise to develop younger players of all sizes, talent levels, backgrounds, and capabilities and inspire them to fall in love with the game of rugby. The players that Coach Bottorff and Coach Enari developed went on to make incredible impacts to the game of rugby through coaching, refereeing, playing for their country, winning national championships, volunteering to lead youth projects—you name it—all for the love of the game. It's a truly indelible legacy.

I confidently stake my claim as being the only rugby player in history to leave a training session early to attend a Norah Jones concert. That's not a Venn Diagram that usually has much overlap, but that's it in terms of what sets me apart from other players. Compared with many of the great players I was lucky enough to meet and play with, my contributions to the sport fall short, but I am most proud that I was able to help get my brother started and had a front row seat watching his progress and development into a sensational player who is leaving his own huge mark on the game.

One of the best speeches I've heard within the game of rugby—and there are many to choose from—came from Scottish coach Jim Telfer, speaking to the British & Irish Lions forwards during a tour in South Africa in 1997.

"There are two types of rugby players," he told the squad. "There's honest ones, and there's the rest."

"The honest player gets up in the morning and looks himself in the mirror and sets his standard. Sets his stall out, and says I'm going to get better. I'm going to get better. I'm going to get better."

"He doesn't complain about the food, or the beds, or buses, or the referees. Or all these sorts of things. These are just peripheral things that weak players have always complained about. The dishonest player."

"What's accepted over there is not accepted over here. It's not accepted by us—me and you. So, from now on the page is turned. We're in a new book, different attitudes. We're honest with ourselves."

I love this because I think it applies to how we can frame an effective mindset in our daily lives in so many different ways—tell the truth, and be honest with yourself about becoming the best version of yourself in your home and at your job and within your community that you can be. Don't make excuses, and don't tolerate yourself or those around you when you or they are being dishonest and giving less than maximum effort.

There are moments when I look back and cannot believe I chose not to play basketball my senior year of high school. But if that thought ever arises, I quickly remember that if I did, there is no chance I would have ever experienced the sport of rugby and all the immense value it has added to my life and my family's life as a result. Without rugby I am not sure I would have met Colleen, and therefore wouldn't have the marriage and kids and life I have today that I cherish so much. I wouldn't have the many adventures I've been able to experience that have been associated with the game, I wouldn't have met the interesting and talented coaches and teammates I have had the privilege to play with, and I wouldn't know this part of the world even existed or how wonderful the culture is. What a shame to think how close I was to missing out on all this goodness.

Doors get closed on us all the time in many ways throughout our lives. One closed for me when I was 18 years old, and at the time the impact of it nearly crushed me. I am grateful another window opened shortly thereafter, and that I had a good friend in Chris Shelley who cared enough to help push me through it. That action impacted more lives than he could have possibly known at the time and changed them for the better.

CHAPTER 35

SOMETIMES REALLY SAD AND AWFUL STUFF HAPPENS

This one hasn't been as much fun to discover as some of the other lessons I have picked up over the years, but I've learned that it doesn't matter where you're from or how much money you have or what kind of home you live in or how much effort and anxiety you actively put forth attempting to avoid misfortune—you will not be spared by the problems life has in store for you, and sometimes flat-out awful things happen to great people who are in no way deserving of it. If anyone suggests there's a solution out there that protects people from the devastating challenges they will face, it is naively misguided at best, and downright deceitful and dangerous at worst.

It would be wonderful if great organizations like St. Jude Children's Hospital, Ronald McDonald Houses, the American Red Cross, and the Make-A-Wish Foundation didn't have to exist. The same goes for Mothers Against Drunk Driving, police and fire departments, and FEMA, to name a few. The dedicated people who work at these places would be thrilled if they woke up tomorrow to find there was literally zero demand for the incredible services they provide to society so they could find a different worthy way to spend their professional lives. But that will not happen. These entities and others like them exist because we need them, and we should be grateful that they're here for us. Sometimes we need them because we're human beings and have flaws that create a negative impact on ourselves and others, and sometimes we need them because through no fault of our own a horrible circumstance shows up at our doorstep and disrupts our life in a devastating way that causes us to require assistance.

By the time you turn 40, there's a good chance you will know a few people who have gone through a variety of deleterious situations, and there's also a good chance you will have experienced a few of them firsthand. You will know people who have lost a loved one too soon to a relentless disease or to a freak accident or to a war or to suicide. You will know people who suffer from addictions and mental illnesses that rob them of the essence that previously made them shine with exquisite brightness. You will know people who have been destitute with no professional prospects on the horizon due to a recession or the collapse of a previously stable organization. Sometimes a tsunami wipes out an entire village with no warning at all, sometimes a massive wildfire engulfs everything in its path, including your home and all your possessions, and sometimes a malevolent maniac drives their car through a Christmas parade filled with children for no reason at all.

Terrible things are happening all over the world, and they're happening all the time. None of this makes any sense to someone dealing with these situations, and sometimes the clarity we're searching for to assuage the pain and confusion seems as if it will never come. There is no *cure* for any of this—tragic situations are going to occur in your life and the lives of your loved ones, and when they do it will be a dark and gloomy and sad and lonely state of existence for just about everyone involved. But I also believe there are many ways we can help each other get through all of it together, and it's worth a try.

We feel helpless when we see people we care about going through pain, but the root of making things just a little bit better can begin with action. When you know someone is going through loss or grief, do what you can to show up for them. Showing up might mean making a phone call to say you're thinking of them and listening to them if they want to talk. It might mean bringing over dinner without being asked, it might mean writing a card or a letter expressing your love and concern for their situation, it might mean giving them a hug or mowing their lawn or sending flowers or offering to watch their kids for an afternoon.

Whatever action looks like, if it's done sincerely and with love, the result is always better than the fear that holds you back because you might mess up the execution or the action will not be "perfect" in the eyes of the receiver. Rest assured, your action to show you care will not be perfect in the eyes of the receiver—they are in immense pain and will be able to focus only on that—but it's *something, and it helps*. Even if the person you're reaching out to has no desire at all to talk with you or doesn't want that hug or screams at you and tells you to get away— their painful reaction has nothing to do with you. Just show up in one way or another and do something kind and thoughtful with the confidence that it will eventually assist, even if only a little. Let them know you're there whenever they're ready.

Not everything can be fixed, mind you. Not all wounds are meant to heal. Nora McInerny is an author and speaker who lost a pregnancy, her father, and her husband all in the span of two months back in 2014. One of the biggest insights she uncovered as she was working her way through her severe grief was that we don't *move on* from that sort of loss…the people we loved and cared so deeply for that are no longer with us do not become a past participle. They remain with us; their joy and their loving memory live with us and we carry them with us forever just as we should. But so does the grief of their loss, and we carry parts of that sadness with us forever too—as we *move forward* in life.

With some losses, we will never move on. But we will move forward, and as we move forward, with any luck we'll discover ways to

Sun 8-8 Unde-PT
Mon
Yvonne 8-8
Tues 8-5 Unde - PT
Weo 8-8 Undes

Which Day H Work

7:3

Dagli Classic Sampler ✳

PT
DOC appt   Shubert + Hwy Cross

GP-8A

Time
flow instead

Dagli Sampler Faster

— Chro —

— Chase —

— St Mikes

Dagli Sampler

(Sub New)

1-8 finding hyyy .

keep ourselves open to love and hope and strength despite the pain that has been experienced. Keep those we love in the present tense for the rest of your days when you speak about them, because their love and their presence remain an eternal part of us…none of it goes away or diminishes after their physical being is no longer here.

I have fallen into deep emotional holes in the past. Whenever I found myself in that type of depressed state, its foundation usually centered on the loss of hope. The loss of hope that whatever I was dealing with at the time was ever going to improve. The loss of hope that I could find a way to recover the goal I was pursuing that ran into an insurmountable roadblock or that failed completely. With time and with small things I did for myself or that others did for me to help, hope slowly started to return. I would notice that while the problems I was facing were real and indeed substantial, I had the ability to get through them and perhaps come out it with a little more resilience and wisdom from the process, no matter how painful it was to deal with.

Whenever I find myself in the middle of a crisis that challenges my outlook and sense of hope, I try to remember the line from Tom Hanks's character in the movie *Cast Away* after enduring a Robinson Crusoe-like journey on an island by himself and living in the harshest mental and physical conditions, completely alone, for four years after surviving a plane crash. After being rescued and getting to return home, he discovers that the wife he had prior to the crash has remarried and now has children of her own because he was assumed dead. Very little about the life he had previously seemed like it was within his reach. He wasn't positive what his next step would be precisely, but within a soliloquy, he said,

"So now I know what I have to do. I have to keep breathing. And tomorrow the sun *will* rise…and who knows what the tide will bring in."

No matter what awful situation you're dealing with, it is never too late for things to change and improve as your life moves forward. Profound grief is real, and when we experience it through the loss of someone or something we care deeply about, it can impact us for the rest of our lives. But hope is real, too, and so is taking small actions to help yourself and others through the storms that show up at our house from time to time. For that to occur, you must stay in the fight. You must show up and be around for it. Because you never know what the tide will bring in.

CHAPTER 36

"ALWAYS TAKE THE HIGH ROAD. IT'S FAR LESS CROWDED."

I heard the saying "Always take the high road. It's far less crowded." for the first time from legendary investor and philanthropist Charlie Munger, the longtime partner of Warren Buffett. Together, they run a company called Berkshire Hathaway—a multinational conglomerate with a market cap in the neighborhood of $650 billion. These two men have attained an otherworldly level of wealth and professional success spanning the course of 60 years and have done so in a manner that would make the words "understated" and "humble" blush with embarrassment. Never have two people led such an enormous entity while flying lower on the radar in their quest to quietly perform their jobs as well as they can for their families, employees, suppliers, partners, and shareholders while trying to avoid the limelight that most executives in their kind of position crave.

Charlie was around age 95, speaking at an annual Daily Journal shareholder meeting in early 2020 and answering questions about business advice and investment strategies. Those in attendance came with the sole purpose of learning anything they could from him. For those who were unfamiliar with Charlie, they likely expected to hear a litany of shrewd and cutthroat principles that set him apart from the competition and the broader market over the course of his career, but that sort of approach has never been his style. He is a disciplined and intelligent person who takes his work incredibly seriously, but he tends to take a more philosophical approach that he explains to others with catchy one-liners that guide his behavior in life and in business.

One trick he's used to give himself and his businesses a competitive edge over the market, which he said was one of the most important reasons his companies succeed, is focused on acting with integrity, keeping your word, delivering the highest potential value for customers, and staying above the fray when others are acting immorally—even if they appear to benefit from it.

He summed this idea up rather succinctly by saying, "Always take the high road. It's far less crowded."

Munger said when taking the high road in business, he chooses to be transparent and ethical in what he sells to people. He wants to sell things that are good for people, rather than tricking them or selling things that are bad for them in the long run.

"I would choose that approach even if I made less money, but in fact, I think you make more." And it's hard to argue with the results his companies have generated.

Munger and Buffett have said that you put yourself at a huge advantage when you choose to take the high road in business, because there aren't too many competitors there. You separate yourself from the crowd. You stand out. You become a trusted partner and someone that others prefer to work with more than their alternatives.

This thinking applies to personal lives as well. When Munger mentions how this approach has led him to make him more money in business, I believe this approach also makes us better partners and friends to others, that it brings more good people into our lives that will be there for us when we need it, and that it leads us to feel prouder of ourselves when we reflect on the journey that's been taken. You will separate yourself as an individual when people see you acting in a manner that promotes integrity and keeping your cool when the time calls for it, which will lead to more people wanting to transact with you in your daily life.

It can be hard taking the high road at times, which is precisely why it's less crowded and why we tend to recognize it so clearly when we see it in action. It's particularly difficult when someone is attacking you with insults and saying things about you that are hurtful and untrue, or when you really want to let your boss have it after you've been unfairly blamed for something that was their mistake. Those are the times you may want to let the beast out and respond angrily with as much vitriol as you just received. There's that false promise you believe that responding with something nasty and hurtful will make you feel better or will somehow even out the score. But Munger's advice about remaining disciplined to stay above the pettiness and instead taking actions that you will be proud of a week, a month, or five years down the road will usually work out much better for you if you can manage it.

I'm not sure there's a single definition that could encapsulate what taking the high road looks like for every situation, but the root of it usually has to do with operating with honesty and not bringing yourself down to the level of those you're interacting with when they choose to act in a manner that you don't believe to be particularly "high" moral or ethical ground.

Taking the high road doesn't mean you accept being treated disrespectfully; it means you respect yourself too much to stoop to their level, demonstrating you're capable of handling your emotions and actions properly when critical situations arise and that you can do the right thing even in the fog of war when others are losing their senses.

Charlie Munger will be the first to tell you that he's been dramatically wrong on a variety of very important decisions he's had to make throughout his illustrative career and life, but I don't think he would point to a single example where he decided to take the high road when given the choice and consider it a mistake—no matter how positive or negative the outcome.

CHAPTER 37

MESSAGE IN A BOTTLE

Stop me if you've heard this one before: Irish guy has thoughts on alcohol consumption.

It's pretty cliché, I know. But I've also had enough experience to develop a point of view and believe it's worth thinking about.

I really enjoy having a bourbon with Colleen as we wind down a long day together. I love drinking a few beers and socializing late into the evening with my friends and family members when we're at a party. Having a cocktail or some wine with dinner is usually a fun thing to include when breaking bread with others. These sorts of activities have been part of my life for a while now.

But I am more aware than when I was younger that it's better to proceed with caution around alcohol, and it's better to proceed with control when making the choice to drink because if left unchecked, the habit is likely to do far more damage than good for me and those around me.

My grandfather came over to the United States from Ireland at age 5 and lived in New Jersey. He met my grandmother there eventually, and they went on to fall in love, get married, and have 11 children together. He served honorably in the military during the Korean War (he also played baseball for the Navy) and was affectionately known as "Dinny." He is the person that my father and I are both named after. He lived a great life and had a significant impact on the people and communities he was a part of.

He was also in Alcoholics Anonymous for 21 years.

I found out about his involvement in AA when I was in middle school and after learning this, I did everything I could to get jersey number 21 in every sport I participated in. I was *proud* to learn that he made that choice to join AA to improve his life and was able to stick with it for so long. He had a small gravestone in the town where I grew up and, occasionally, I would ride my bike to go clean it off and pay my respects, and whenever I did, I always loved seeing the AA logo with the triangle inside a circle inscribed with the number 21.

My Uncle Tom, one of Dinny's sons, came to the realization that alcohol was not positively contributing to his marriage or his relationship with his kids, and he made the choice to live without it. He has now been sober for 15 years and has become a tremendous role model whom I look up to, not just because he quit drinking, but because of what kind of person he has become as a result of his sobriety and the dedication he put forth to make it a reality.

My Uncle Tom shows up to every family event. He calls to check in to say hello and asks how I am doing. He is available to offer advice whenever I need it. He is thoughtful and kind and hardworking and has raised incredible children. He has become a pillar for his family and for his community.

If you ask him, none of these positive developments in his life would have happened if he had not stopped drinking.

Dinny, Tom, and others like them deserve credit for acknowledging that things weren't going well across a variety of areas as a result of their drinking and having the courage and discipline to make a meaningful change in their lives. That change took time and took some serious self-analysis, but it ultimately made their lives far better than the alternative. Which in turn made their spouse's life better. And their children's lives better. And their communities better. These changes had an impact on generations to come, because the positive course correction was so strong and so far-reaching.

I've learned that if alcohol, like anything else, is a contributing force that is consistently making your life worse, it would be prudent to take an honest look at the environments and emotions you're dealing with that lead you to consistently choose to use it. If the use of alcohol limits your ability to be relied on by your family, friends, and professional circles, if it is diminishing your health, if it is straining your relationships, if it is leading to getting into trouble with the law, if it is taking you further from the habits you believe make you a stronger and better version of yourself, if it's being used as a distraction to avoid the difficult challenges and responsibilities you're facing—it's best to take measures to limit its presence in your life.

I don't believe there is virtue in abstinence alone when it comes to alcohol—the presence of alcohol doesn't automatically make people bad, and its absence doesn't automatically make people good. But if abstinence from alcohol helps you live in a stronger, more responsible, more capable manner, and if abstinence reduces your proclivity to engage in damaging thoughts and behaviors, then that would seem to be a good thing for you and everyone around you.

I do know that the times I have felt most embarrassed or regretful or ashamed of what I said or how I acted in my 20's and 30's often involved alcohol—and had I not been drinking on those occasions, it's likely that I would have behaved in a more responsible manner.

When I am stressed, I've learned that working out or going to yoga is a better tool to calm me down and get me back on track than ripping shots of Fireball.

When I am dealing with sadness and grief, I've learned that doing so without drinking too much allows me to feel the depths of whatever it is I am going through and to eventually find acceptance, rather than covering it up on the surface and not addressing the core issue.

I want to teach my kids how to handle alcohol properly, because it will be a constant presence in their lives as students, as professionals, and in the social gatherings they participate in, and it's better to be aware than naïve. I want to make sure they know that the party scene will always be there waiting for you, and not to sacrifice the interests and goals you have in high school and college or throughout your professional career that will not always be there.

There have been countless fun memories I have made with family and friends that involved alcohol throughout the past two decades, and I look forward to many more with my friends and my children as they get old enough to partake. But I also want to ensure that there is structure and guidance that my children and I understand around its presence in our lives, and the belief that "balance is key" is a pretty good way to remember that alcohol shouldn't become *everything*.

CHAPTER 38

LIVE WITHIN YOUR MEANS

I visited China in 2011 during a business trip and stopped at one of those markets you often hear about where knockoff North Face Jackets and Prada Handbags sell for $10 apiece and begin falling apart before you get to the parking lot. Instead of Air Jordans, you might see a pair of Error Jordans being sold at a market like this. You get the idea.

The co-workers I was traveling with had been coming to this market for many years and always made a habit of stopping at one shop that didn't have any signage out front or many employees that could be found on entering the doors. They walked confidently to a counter located in the back of store and rang the bell.

"Is Jason working?" they asked inconspicuously. "We're here to see the watches."

When I looked around the store, I saw tons of unofficially manufactured Burberry scarves, Polo shirts, and thousands of bootleg DVD's from what appeared to be every American television sitcom ever created. I did not, however, see any watches, so I was confused who Jason was and what he could possibly have to do with watches.

There was hesitancy from the store clerk on being prompted but his concern subsided when one of my co-workers said, "Rolex" while pointing to his wrist highlighting a huge watch that I hadn't noticed up to that point. When the employee saw the watch, he lifted the latch on the counter and walked us into a different room located behind the back wall.

"This way," was all he said, and we followed him toward the hidden destination in total silence.

I don't think I even owned a watch before this trip, so I wasn't exactly sure what I was looking at when we walked into Jason's Lair, but I knew it had to be special after seeing my co-workers become giddy and start talking excitedly to one another about how impressive the selection was that lined the massive display that was uncovered to us.

I saw that every single one of the co-workers I was with had an impressive looking watch on their wrist and realized this was the place where they'd been purchased over the years. After fumbling my way around for a while, I fell for the peer pressure and ended up paying $50 for a cool looking large black watch that I'd never heard of before that I thought would match the Old Navy jeans and tee shirts I wore around the house most weekends.

When we left the store and the coast was clear, I pulled the watch from my pack to show my boss who started beaming with pride. "Oh-ho-hoo…That's a $30,000 Hublot watch, Dennis. Nice choice indeed—people are going to think you're the man when you walk into your next meeting!"

My stomach sunk.

The real version of this thing cost thirty thousand post-tax U.S. dollars? For a watch?

I drive a ten-year-old Jeep with 150,000 miles on it. My wife has had the same beat-up Mitsubishi Lancer she's been driving since college that is falling apart in every way conceivable. I am currently *renting* a home in a modest neighborhood. I have a 1-year-old baby and my wife is pregnant with our second child. I mow my own lawn because I don't want to give the neighbor kid $20 to do it every week. I buy lunch at the Spinx Gas Station down the street from our office most days.

Remind me again why I would ever want anyone to think I *actually spent* $30,000 on a Hublot watch. Would any of that make sense? And if anyone knew about my true financial state at that time and believed that I purchased a $30K watch, my boss thought that their first reaction would be that "I am the man!?"

This was not good.

Thankfully one of the hands on the watch stopped working before I returned home to Greenville, South Carolina, so I never actually had a reason to wear it in public—but as soon as I heard the price tag I knew this watch was not something I wanted to showcase, because I definitely didn't want to mistakenly imply to anyone else I had that kind of money to blow on a watch, or even worse that I didn't have that kind of money but still decided to buy a $30K watch.

I've learned that spending more money than you have so you can chase status, or cope with an emotional void, or try to impress others will lead to an unfulfilling, stressful, and dangerous way of living. Living within my means and being diligent when it comes to saving and spending money, even when there isn't very much to go around, has led to a more authentic lifestyle and has put me in a better position to take advantage of more opportunities as they arise in the future.

I've noticed that living within my means has brought more peace, stability, and honesty to my life than spending money I don't have trying to gain favor with people I don't care about, with designer clothes and fancy cars to try to make myself seem like something I am not. When I make the decision to live within my means, it also attracts the type of people that share similar values, which makes it more fun for me to engage with them because there isn't as much concern about the things we feel don't matter. I don't mind sharing Costco Kirkland brand wine with people when they come to my house for dinner, because it's delicious and I don't think it's that different from more expensive wines with prestigious brands. If you don't like Costco Kirkland wine, that's fine—we all have our preferences. But if you think my serving it at the house makes me something "less" in your eyes, it's likely that we aren't aligned in a few other important areas when it comes to spending money, or projecting an image, and how we allow others' perceptions to impact our actions.

Living within your means doesn't mean settling for less. If you've got goals to make a ton of money, that's great—go out and make a ton of money. If you want to go out and accumulate tons of fancy things because they bring you joy, that's awesome. I just think it's way harder to achieve those goals if you're consistently spending more money than you make along the way, if you aren't being disciplined when it comes to saving, and it's likely that the journey itself becomes a little less enjoyable when you're putting an image out to the world that doesn't reflect your reality.

Morgan Housel is an American business and finance journalist who wrote a book titled "The Psychology of Money." I consider it the best thing I have read when it comes to understanding people's behaviors, fears, and mindsets around all things money because of its directness and ease of comprehension. The lessons communicated in the book are not a post-graduate course on microeconomics or a detailed look at the world of derivatives; they are an easy-to-read guide that helps you frame why you see money the way you do and why you behave the way you do regarding your saving and spending habits. There are suggestions on ways we can break free from the chains we place on ourselves when we try to impress others, when we take financial advice from people who have misaligned incentives and goals, etc., and he provides insights on how to better understand the magic of compounding interest. His book makes it clear that it's not so much the amount of money you earn, it's how much money you spend relative to your earnings that can be one of the most significant contributors to long-term financial stability.

No matter how much money I ever accumulate in my life, I will still look at the bottom line and think, "Yeah but there should definitely be

50 more bucks on top that I wasted at some knockoff chop shop watch closet in Shanghai. You win, Jason. You win."

Live within your means. Saving money is better than wasting money. Sacrifice spending today so that tomorrow can be better. Take control of your financial acumen. No one will do any of this for you, so the sooner you develop good habits and a healthy mindset around money, the better it will be for you and those that eventually rely on you.

CHAPTER 39

"I WISH I COULD DO IT ALL OVER AGAIN."

I misunderstood a comment from a family member that stopped me in my tracks recently and thought it was worthy of sharing and remembering.

Colleen has a grandmother who is close to 90 years old and lives near us, and we wanted to bring the kids over to say hello, since it had been a while since we'd last seen her. Her name is Margaret, which is also the name of one of our daughters, and the two of them always share great excitement together knowing that they have that in common with each other.

When we visited her at home she was as upbeat and talkative as ever even though she hadn't seen many people over the past six months due to COVID. Most of her daily routines and activities had been completely halted earlier that year, and although COVID wasn't easy for anyone to go through, I have to imagine it was particularly difficult for older people who found themselves isolated and alone for longer periods of time than they were accustomed to like Great Grandma Margaret.

We talked with her for hours that afternoon about the events that had been transpiring across the world and getting caught up with each other. When she found out that our daughter Evelyn was working on a school project that was based on family members serving in the military, we pored through the archives of pictures and binders filled with newspaper clippings and artifacts that she'd kept from her husband Patrick's time serving honorably in the 28th Infantry Division of the US Army in the 1940s during World War II.

Our children learned about their great grandfather's experience in the Battle of the Bulge, which took place in Belgium and was won by U.S. and Allied Forces and essentially ended any German chances of victory in the war. We discussed the various decorations and recognitions he earned throughout his service, like Bronze Battle Stars and Good Conduct Medals. We listened to how he performed his role as a surgical technician when he was first onboarded overseas. It was a beautiful conversation between a great grandmother and five of her great grandchildren, and each person was grateful to be in each other's company that afternoon.

As people age and approach the end of their lives, you sometimes hear them talk more about the regrets they have, what they wished they'd done differently, and what they would do instead if given the chance to start again. These can be difficult conversations to hear someone think through, because there can be a tremendous amount of pain and remorse that's prevalent in the heart and mind of the speaker and there isn't a whole lot you can do as a listener, aside from lending a caring ear to provide comfort and assurance. I had first met Great Grandma Margaret 12 years before this visit and never once thought that she was the type of person to hold onto those kinds of feelings or harbor any sense of regret about how her life turned out, but you never really know—and we were having the kind of open and honest conversations with each other that day during which a window might open for us to cover something like that together. It's obviously not something you want to lead with or suggest, but it's also a conversation you would agree to have if an elder family member you were speaking with decided to go in that direction.

We completed our deep-dive into Great Grandpa Patrick's military history, and eventually the kids heard a few more fun stories and about the adventures Patrick and Margaret had shared together throughout their 60+ year marriage. It was around this time that I noticed Great Grandma took a long breath that seemed both reflective and serious, but her tone didn't quite match what I thought I was seeing in the facial expressions.

"Uh-oh," I thought to myself. Here it comes.

"I wish I could do it all over again..." she said.

And for a *split second* I thought my assumption was right. For a split second I thought this was going to be a sad conversation about what would be done differently if given the chance, and one we would sit back and listen to with love as she worked through whatever it was she needed to.

But I quickly noticed that she didn't say this in a way that I'd heard anyone her age express a thought like that before, and it certainly wasn't said in a way that I was expecting. This was a *joyful* message. This was *hopeful*. This was beautiful and strong and was charged with appreciation.

She burst into a huge smile and smacked the table with her hand as she continued, "I wish I could do it all over again because my life has just been the best! I had the best parents, I had the best childhood, I had the best marriage, I had the best kids, and I had the best family. If I could do it all over again I would do it just the same. Every bit of it." We then listened to her speak about how wonderful her mother was and the loving memories she held of her, how much she adored the unique traits each of her three children, and how much joy they had brought into her life, and how proud she was of all the families her three children had grown of their own.

I loved every part of that explanation, and it was clear that she meant it. She was expressing so much gratitude and appreciation for the people and opportunities that she'd come across in her life—which isn't to say things had never gone wrong or that she didn't suffer in pain at times or endure extremely challenging periods—but the gratitude for the goodness and love she'd experienced outweighed everything else to the point that if given the chance to go back in time and have complete control, not one thing would be different. That's a helluva thing to feel after 90 years, when you think about it.

Frederick Nietzsche wrote about an ancient Greek theory called Eternal Recurrence, also called Eternal Return, which holds that all events in the world repeat themselves in the same sequence through an eternal series of cycles. Whatever takes place in the life you're leading now—whatever challenges you face, whatever shortcomings you have, whatever pain and suffering and anxieties you endure—the premise states that you are destined to repeat them in the same fashion with no chance of improving on them following the conclusion of the life you're living now.

In discussing the idea of Eternal Recurrence, it is believed that Nietzsche's intention was not to submit the idea as truth, but to inspire us to ask ourselves how we would think and act if the idea were true. It is designed to help people identify whether they feel they are on the right track and living in a manner that they find fulfilling and meaningful. If you think you're doing well in these areas and are asked to ponder the idea of Eternal Recurrence, you may not have much concern when this theory is presented to you to consider. If you're in a particularly bad place and know that the life you're living has been far short of what would be considered close to your ideal state of being, this thought experiment about it repeating throughout all of eternity is about as terrifying as it gets.

Life is going to be filled with moments of pain, and loss, and suffering, and mistakes, and malevolence, and stress, and other awful emotions that we would prefer to exit as quickly as possible and hopefully not have to experience again in the future.

But I love that during our conversation, Great Grandma Margaret looked at the "Eternal Recurrence" of her life and basically said, "This is awesome; sign me up!"

Her answer caught me by surprise in the best possible way, and it's a mindset I have thought about ever since I heard her say it.

CHAPTER 40

CONCLUSION

4O stories, sayings, and lessons-learned covering 40 years. That's all there is to say, right?

Fin.

No mas.

Done-zo.

Except…it isn't.

It's impossible to convey all the impactful experiences we encounter in a way that makes any sense, especially within a book. These have been just a few of the snippets and thoughts that were meaningful to my life that I wanted to think through in more detail and write out as a milestone birthday was on the horizon. The writings I selected for this book were also ones I believed others might relate to and learn something about their own lives from. There is no ranking or hierarchy to the stories that have been shared, and there are plenty of important topics and ideas and experiences and people that have influenced my life that were not covered at all.

There is some risk writing a book like this. There is fear of putting yourself out there and leaving yourself open to critique from family members, acquaintances, and strangers alike. There are people who will undoubtedly misinterpret something I've said or eventually attempt to use this book against me when I find myself in a challenging situation, as if to say happily to me, "Well hey, guess you shouldn't have written that book then, huh?!"

Let me just beat those people to the punch and say this: I am going to make a ton more mistakes in the future. I will look like a fool many more times in the future from my actions and from my inactions. There will be many occasions when I don't have all the answers in the future. The mistakes I make may even go against a few of the tenets I wrote about in this book.

But worrying about any of that is a pretty dumb reason to stop you from doing something you care about. And somewhere within me, I have wanted to write a book for a long time. I don't know exactly where that desire came from, and I never knew what form it would take, but it has been there for a while and as soon as the idea to write this book was born in my mind, it became impossible for me to shake. Rather than suppressing and worrying about the thought, I developed an outline of themes I wanted to think through and eventually identified the ideas that I most wanted to write about and decided to give them a little room to breathe.

One of the themes I hope was properly conveyed throughout this book is gratitude. More than 2,000 years ago, Cicero said, "Gratitude is not only the greatest of the virtues; it is the parent of all the others." I believe that sentiment remains wise and true today. I've learned that I don't have to be grateful *for* all situations—because after all, who could be grateful for the pain and loss and suffering we experience when it comes our way? But I can be grateful *in* all situations and carry the understanding that there are blessings in my life and beauty within the world I can appreciate and hold onto when wading through challenging times. I've been so lucky to meet many wonderful people in my life and am grateful for the privilege to call them my family and my friends.

Another theme I wanted to convey is that we can make things better for ourselves and for those around us. Don't wait for someone else to do it. Don't think that the big actions are the ones that matter most. You are far more capable of enacting change than you may believe. Start with yourself, start with something small that you can control, and get going. The more action you take, the more you will find is possible. Confidence will come from preparation and practice. Action might be as simple as giving a smile to someone who is difficult to work with to improve a relationship, or as complex as working your way out of the brink of financial and emotional ruin—but there are actions you can take today to make things ever so slightly better than they were yesterday, and over time they can make a world of difference.

Others' truths do not have to be your own. What worked for someone else may not work for you, and vice versa. Find out for yourself what you believe to be true about yourself and the world around you. There are people out there who genuinely love you and want the best for you who will do their best to provide the sincerest advice they can provide, and there are times you might discover that their direction is not for you. It doesn't mean you don't love them, and it doesn't mean they're wrong. It just means that sometimes you must discover things on your own.

Beauty can be found anywhere. The same can be said for wisdom and ingenuity and grit when your eyes and mind are open to it, so don't limit yourself by only looking for it in the people and places you have a preconceived notion it will be present. These qualities aren't limited by an individual's zip code or income level or educational background or in the way they speak and look. You won't find more of it in Manhattan, New York City, and you won't find less of it in Manhattan, Illinois. Everyone you meet is going through something. They're all living out their own stories and have their own baggage and background and accomplishments and needs that they bring into every situation. Have some empathy and try to learn what you can from them along the way.

Nurture ten people in your life that truly love you; that will be far more meaningful and fulfilling than having ten million people that merely like you. Depending on your position, you may be able to force someone else to listen to you or force them to like you or even follow you—but you cannot force someone else to respect you. Respect must be earned, and a good way to start is by showing others a little respect first.

Above all, what I want to convey to my wife and children in this book and through my actions moving forward is that you are the greatest gifts I could have ever asked for in this lifetime, and I love and cherish you more than I can possibly explain.

To Colleen: when I was writing these stories, I was able to take stock of my past and realized there were about a million ways I almost never met you, given how different my life was before we came together. But I also know without question that you're part of the destiny I was born to live out, and there is nothing that could have kept us apart. I know how special all of this is and how lucky we are to have each other, so I want to focus my life around making it the best we can for each other as we continue to grow together with the wonderful family we've created.

To our children: my goal as your father is to provide you with the utmost love and security so you have the confidence to move forward and bring the best out of yourself. To encourage you. To give you the tools to learn how to maximize the greatness and potential you have within you in whatever you decide you want to do in this life. To make sure you are prepared and strong and willing to take on the challenges you'll encounter on your own path.

The truth is, I have no idea what the *best* piece advice is to give you if I had to choose one—you will change, your temperament will change, the world will change, and there will be many different nuggets of wisdom you'll come across that will be more useful than others at different points in your life.

You'll soon pass milestones like middle school and high school graduation, you may go off to college, get a job, have some adventures, fall down, get up, fall down again, and get back up again. You may meet a spouse, have some babies, raise those babies, and so much more. You're going to meet friends, lose friends, find new parts of yourself and leave other parts behind. And I will want to be next to you along every single step of the way with the same goal of wanting to be the best possible father I can be, in whatever capacity you need me. Our roles will begin to change soon, just as they subtly have been shifting on a daily basis since you began taking on more intellectual capacity, the ability to look after yourself more, and learning how to be responsible and accountable for yourselves. That's a good thing, too. Just know that no matter what shifts take place or what paths you take or what changes occur—I will be here as your father, as your mom's husband, and we will always be with you and love you.

No matter what amazing accomplishments you go on to achieve in your life, no matter where you find yourself in this world—never forget how happy you've made me as your father, how you've made me and your mom the proudest parents imaginable, and how much joy you've provided to those around you—you have our hearts forever and we will always, always love you.

—Dennis O'Donnell

Let us agree that we shall never forget one another. And whatever happens, let us remember how good it felt when we were all here together united by a good and decent feeling, which made us better people — better probably than we would otherwise have ever been.

Father Theodore Hesburgh, former president
of the University of Notre Dame

Should this 11 year old have been in school on the morning of November 12, 1993? Probably. But getting the chance to see Lou Holtz in person before the big Florida State game was simply too awesome of an opportunity to pass up.

From Chapter 2 – *Lessons From Lou*

Joe, Allen, Chris, and me at Zion National Park
From Chapter 5 – *Go Find An Adventure*

Me and Colleen at the summit of Mount Quandary
From Chapter 5 – *Go Find An Adventure*

No chance this photo of our family is possible if Colleen and her friends were able to get their hands on a ticket similar to the one shown above on August 31, 2008
From Chapter 8 – *August 31, 2008*

From Chapter 9 – *I Love Watching You Play*

From Chapter 10 – *Outside Is Better Than Inside*

Julius and Pops together at The B&B
From Chapter 11 – *Pocket Tens, As People*

Jumping to 1 on our wedding day
From Chapter 12 – *Going From 0 To 1 Is A Bigger Jump Than 1 To 6*

Sneaking in a quick a smooch in front of our obviously thrilled children
From Chapter 12 – *Going From 0 To 1 Is A Bigger Jump Than 1 To 6*

One of our favorite family pictures from our time together in Atlanta
From Chapter 14 – *Georgia On Our Mind*

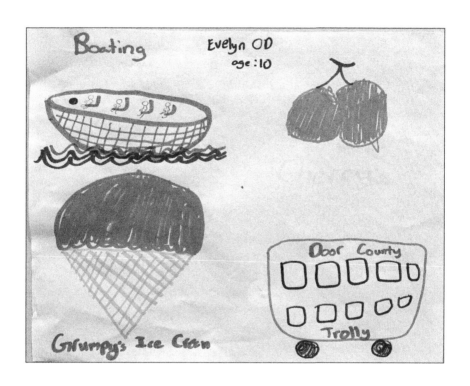

From Chapter 16 – *Once Upon A Time In Door County*

My sister, Shannan, with The Great Dog Sophie
From Chapter 17 – *Thank You Pat Conroy. And Susannah.*

If riding a tandem bike around the neighborhood in lederhosen doesn't scream "cool" then I don't know what does
From Chapter 21 – *If You Can Ride A Bike, Go Ride A Bike*

We live in an amazing town and are grateful for all the wonderful people
we've met since moving here
From Chapter 25 – *Thank You, Wheaton*

From Chapter 25 – *Thank You, Wheaton*

Grams and her crew

From Chapter 27 – *The Power Of A Praying Mother*

From Chapter 33 – *The Greatest Book Ever Written*

A former professional rugby player, and his older brother
From Chapter 37 – *Windows, Doors, And Rugby Tours*

ADVANCE PRAISE FOR 40 FOR 40

"Seriously? I told him writing this book was a really dumb idea, but it looks like he went ahead and did it anyways. This was not a great use of his time, nor a good use of my time. Sinfully bad."

— Pope Francis

"I've read better literature that was written on the side of a bathroom stall. And I'm not talking about stalls in one of those fancy gas stations, the ones with the showers in them and stuff. I'm talking about the bad gas stations where you need a key to get into the restrooms. Those stalls. It's a real shame this guy is from Indiana."

— Larry Bird

"When I create the next version of human robots, I am going to equip them with more than two hands so they can give this book the appropriate number of 'thumbs down' that it deserves."

— Elon Musk

"I liked it. But I can't really read yet. So maybe you should ask someone else? I'm hungry, where's mom?"

— Danny O'Donnell, Age 5